Quality Pays

Increasing Profits

Through

Quality Cost Analysis

John J. Heldt
and
Daniel J. Costa

Hitchcock Publishing Company
Wheaton, Illinois 60188

Library of Congress Catalog Number 88-81167

John J. Heldt & Daniel J. Costa
        Quality Pays

First Edition
©1988 by Hitchcock Publishing Company, Wheaton, IL 60188
Loren M. Walsh, President

Capital Cities/ABC Inc. company

    Editorial Supervision: Raymond J. Kimber. Editor: Virgil J. Busto
    Cover Design: Steve Falco
    Production: Annette Mola, Lisbeth Schar, Bev Morris, Joan Wilder,
    Arlene Bartolini, Marie Ary, Charles Doyle

Printed in the United States of America

10   9   8   7   6   5   4   3   2   1

ISBN 0-933931-07-7

PREFACE

As American industry rolls along the winding, and often tricky, recovery path on its way into the 1990s and the 21st century, it is clear that our greatest challenges are still ahead. Foreign competition shows no sign of diminishing. American industry needs a major change in strategy to successfully maneuver up this path strewn with pitfalls and relics of the past. For some, such as the automotive industry, the transformation is already well underway. For the rest of us the transformation has just begun.

Guidance to determine the critical elements we need for the coming transformation comes from the auto industry. Ford's "Quality Is Job One" and Chrysler's ability to extend warranties and lower sticker prices due to improved production methods give us excellent insight. Quality products can be sold at lower prices because less material and labor are wasted on scrap and rework. This seems to be the focal point of the auto industry's efforts, and so it must be for the rest of American industry.

In short, the ability and willingness of foreign competitors to provide both American and worldwide consumers with quality products at cost-effective prices have brought many segments of American industry to their knees. To regain lost markets and the competitive edge, industry must approach the challenge in much the same way our competitors did in the 1950s, 1960s and 1970s. We must learn (or in some cases, relearn) how to improve the quality and productivity of our manufacturing processes. We will have to apply all the tools and techniques available to us: some borrowed from competitors and some resurrected from our past. But most importantly, American industry must commit itself to the aggressive and unyielding pursuit of quality improvement, thus significantly reducing the cost of scrap and rework.

The measurement and control of the costs associated with quality are major steps down the road to recovery. It is to this endeavor that this book is dedicated.

Though the concepts associated with cost of quality are not new, relatively few companies within American industry have been able to implement them, and even fewer fully understand them. In the following chapters the authors have made a thorough presentation of these concepts in order that you will be able to understand, implement and benefit from the improved quality and reduced costs that will result.

Both authors have reduced the cost of quality in their own plants using the principles shown here. Both have been able to convince accountants and management alike by showing spectacular results. You may find the going tough, especially at first, but keep at it . . . the results will be well worth your efforts!

CONTENTS

Preface iii

List of Figures vi

BOOK ONE Quality Pays 1
Chapter 1 Profit Improvement through
                 Quality/Productivity 3
Chapter 2 The Quality Cost Procedure 11
Chapter 3 Categories of Quality Costs 14
Chapter 4 Collection of Quality Costs 19
Chapter 5 Analysis of Quality Costs 25
Chapter 6 The Cost of Quality Report 35
Chapter 7 Organizing and Managing for Improvement. . . . 44
Chapter 8 Tuning the Quality Cost System for Added Profit . 52
Chapter 9 Postscript: Reducing White Collar Overhead . . . 61
                 Afterword 66
Appendix A Quality Cost Worksheets 68
Appendix B Sample Cost of Quality Procedure 71
Appendix C Quality Cost Account Structure 74
                 Bibliography and Recommended Reading. 84

BOOK TWO The Quality Cost Workbook 85
Section I Life Cycle Costs 86
Section II Cost of Quality Exercises 91
Section III Pareto Analyses and Matrices 101
Section IV Cost of Quality Analyses 108

Appendix I Life Cycle Costs Answers and Comments 122
Appendix II Cost of Quality Exercise Answers
                 and Comments 127
Appendix III Pareto Analyses and Matrices Answers 135
Appendix IV Cost of Quality Analyses Answers and Comments . 144
                 Index 155

LIST OF FIGURES

Figure No.	Description	Page No.
1	Doubling and Redoubling Your Profit	5
2	Operational Quality Costs	7
3	Overhead Worksheet	23
4	Pareto Analysis 1	26
5	Week One	27
6	Week Two	27
7	Pareto Analysis 2	28
8	Defect Descriptions (and Code Numbers)	28
9	Matrix	29
10	Defect Descriptions (Codes and Costs included)	29
11	Matrix	29
12	Cover Letter to Management	37
13	Detailed Cost Summary	38
14	Total Cost of Quality Trend Chart	39
15	Major Cost of Quality Trend Chart	40
16	Total Cost of Quality Trend Chart	54
17	Major Cost of Quality Trend Chart	55
18	Total Cost of Quality Trend Chart	56
19	Major Cost of Quality Trend Chart	57
20	Total Cost of Quality Trend Chart	58
21	Major Cost of Quality Trend Chart	59
22	Chart of Accounts	64

BOOK ONE

Quality Pays

CHAPTER 1

Profit Improvement through Quality/Productivity

It is no secret that American industry is in deep trouble. Low productivity levels and foreign competition are just two of the many factors that are threatening our economic stability, our standard of living and the individual images that each of us hold which can collectively be described as "the American dream."

One of the images that Americans held high for so long was that if it's American-made then it's made better. But each of us knows, in spite of the current TV campaign, the label "Made in the U.S.A." no longer guarantees a better-made product. We've all personally experienced the myriad products that fail and we've learned that the warranty simply guarantees us a place in a long repair line.

While we're standing in line with our product that needs repairing, does it occur to us that our product may not get fixed? If it wasn't made right the first time, where do we get the idea a revolution is going to take place the second time around?

Did we ever have the right to the idea that American products were better, or were we merely the instrument for showing everyone else how to do it so they could take over our industries, one by one? If we ever deserved the leadership position, will we ever again earn the right to say "American-made is better" or will it remain a falsely reassuring TV campaign?

If the images we once held of America as a country with the highest standard of living, as a model of freedom and a teacher of leading technology are ever going to ring true again, every American is going to have to realize our falling standard of living is our own fault. We can't blame it on foreign competition. We can't blame it on our government, or on our president or which party controls Congress. It isn't only the *other* fellow's productivity that's down.

With the help of W. Edwards Deming, known as the "Father of Japanese Quality," Japan learned that they couldn't build a first-rate economy with second-rate products. Americans knew this at one time but we seem to have forgotten that the simplest and least costly means of increasing both productivity and profits is to *improve quality.* If you make a product that satisfies a need and it doesn't require repairing, rejecting or recalling, then quality doesn't *cost,* it *pays* you back.

It should be obvious that rework due to poor design or workmanship increases product cost. Or that, for example, the cost of an assembly will double if half of the production has to be scrapped.

Deming makes this effect much clearer when he describes his Quality—Productivity Chain. Simplified, the Quality—Productivity Chain is described as follows:

• *Better quality (making it right every time) brings the result of better productivity.* This is true because less (or no) time is used for rework or for building units to be salvaged—hence the productivity increases because 100 percent of the manufacturing time is devoted to making the product.

• *Better productivity brings greater customer satisfaction.* It means schedules are met, costs are in line and the quality is good.

• *Greater customer satisfaction brings more business,* which in turn makes the company more profitable, which in turn makes the employees more efficient which results in even better quality—productivity consciousness—and thus the chain continues.

For a long time, our government has seen the need to tabulate our quality costs. The following quotation is from MIL-Q-9858A Quality Program Requirements, Section 3. Quality Program Management:

> *COSTS RELATED TO QUALITY. The contractor shall maintain and use quality cost data as a management element of the quality program. These data shall serve the purpose of identifying the cost of both the prevention and correction of nonconforming supplies (e.g., labor and material involved in material spoilage caused by defective work, correction of defective work and for quality control exercised by the contractor at subcontractor's or vendor's facilities). The specific quality cost data to be maintained and used will be determined by the contractor. These data shall, on request, be identified and made available for "on site" review by the government representative.*

Many contractors to the government simply total the salaries and wages of their quality people and the cost of other quality department incidentals and submit the total as their "quality cost." When the government representative points this out to be inadequate, the contractor's representative quotes from the paragraph above, "The specific quality cost data to be maintained and used will be determined by the contractor." Defense Contract Administrative Services (DCAS) representatives are beginning a "get tough" policy with these contractors, but so far not much headway has been made.

It should be recognized that many manufacturers (all those who believe that "good quality is good business") do maintain and use quality cost data as a management element of the quality program, whether they are contractors to the government or not.

Since the idea of moving the cost of quality into the profit column is the basic premise for any quality cost program, let us consider the following example and subsequent illustration in Figure 1:

A manufacturing company with $10 million in annual sales has a cost of quality equal to 10 percent of gross sales ($1 million) and a profit of 2 percent ($0.2 million). To double the company's profit will require only a 20 percent improvement in the cost of quality, an objective that can be easily achieved in almost any manufacturing company that does not already have a cost of quality program in place. To understand how significant this really is, one need only consider that to achieve the same results through growth in sales would require a 100 percent increase during the same period required to effect the cost of quality improvement—a very unlikely circumstance. Further, even if sales could be increased within the time required, the company would still show only a meager 2 percent profit since no real improvements were made—increases in profit

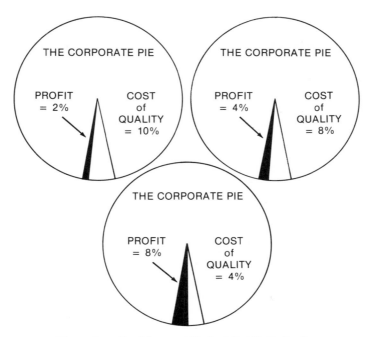

Figure 1 — Doubling and Redoubling Your Profit

dollars would simply be the result of increased volumes.

The best part is that a 40 percent improvement (resulting in a 6 percent profit) in the cost of quality is more likely than stopping at the 20 percent (4 percent profit) mark.

Operating Costs

Operational quality costs are divided into the costs of quality control and the costs of lack of quality control. These two major divisions of costs are briefly described here and charted in Figure 2.

COSTS OF QUALITY CONTROL

Appraisal Cost

Appraisal cost includes the costs of all inspection and test, calibration, maintenance of test equipment and the like.

Prevention Cost

Prevention cost includes the costs of quality management, training and such. The ratio between this cost and the cost of appraisal should be about 1 to 4. One rule of thumb indicates that your management of quality costs is approaching optimum when the total of both these categories is about half of the total of all of the quality costs.

COSTS OF LACK OF QUALITY CONTROL

Internal Failure Cost

Internal failure cost is typically made up of scrap cost, rework costs—including reinspection and retesting—and any other costs that can be attributed to lack of quality control prior to final acceptance of the product.

External Failure Cost

External failure cost includes warranty costs as well as field engineering and field failure costs. Typically, these costs are expected to be 90 percent of the total failure costs (cost of lack of quality control), if for no other reason than the added expenses involved in dealing with failures in the field. *(See Summary, Item 2, page 60.)*

The ensuing chapters will deal exclusively with the operating quality cost concept. The rest of this chapter will be devoted to other quality concepts and the cost involved with them.

Design Quality

One of the factors that makes everyone believe that good quality

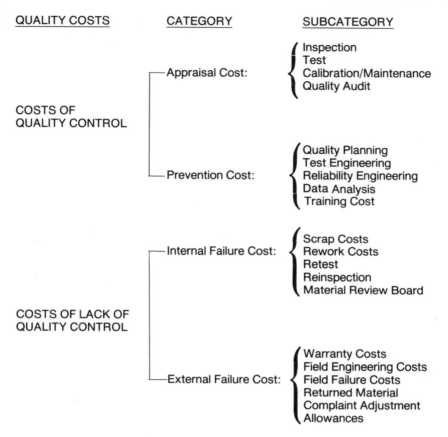

QUALITY COSTS   CATEGORY   SUBCATEGORY

Appraisal Cost:
{ Inspection
Test
Calibration/Maintenance
Quality Audit

COSTS OF
QUALITY CONTROL

Prevention Cost:
{ Quality Planning
Test Engineering
Reliability Engineering
Data Analysis
Training Cost

Internal Failure Cost:
{ Scrap Costs
Rework Costs
Retest
Reinspection
Material Review Board

COSTS OF LACK OF
QUALITY CONTROL

External Failure Cost:
{ Warranty Costs
Field Engineering Costs
Field Failure Costs
Returned Material
Complaint Adjustment
Allowances

Figure 2 — Operational Quality Costs

costs more involves the cost of design quality. The classic example of design quality being more expensive is the comparison of the luxury car to the less costly car that everyone "knows" is cheaper because it is lower quality. Unfortunately, conformance to specification or fitness for use is not considered in this concept. It doesn't matter that the less expensive car is as safe or will last as long as the luxury car (i.e., that the design is good and the workmanship and quality control assure that it is put together right). What does matter is the extra room in the luxury car, the quieter ride, the larger engine and the oversize tires—and all of these *do* cost more money. We should substitute "luxury" or "prestige" instead of "quality" for most of the differences.

Design quality is the factor that makes the advertised "best" category the most expensive and the "good" category the cheapest. This factor also gets us in trouble when we try to find out where our operating costs are coming from. We need to find out where we stand and eventually to bring them to an optimum figure. To do this we must learn to differentiate between the costs brought about by a more elaborate design and the costs involved in making sure that our product conforms to that design.

Since the major task of this analysis revolves around the balancing of the costs of control of quality against the costs of failure of quality control, we must start from the premise that our design meets the customer's needs. We must remember that good quality is less expensive than poor quality. We must remember that the product can be designed to greater or lesser luxury and realize that these factors make the cost of the product higher or lower. Our major effort must be to optimize the operating quality costs that are needed to make sure that we are conforming to our design specifications.

Life Cycle Costs

One other type of quality cost that should be discussed is life cycle cost. This is sometimes called use cost. This is the type of cost that is discussed in terms of "It is cheaper to buy a Mercedes that costs three times as much because it will outlast five Volkswagens." Usually, this statement is followed by words to the effect that you had best be certain that you like the model, since you may be driving it for a long time. This is usually followed by another statement to the effect that you will always be driving a "quality" automobile.

Another variation is the sales claim that the electronic ignition furnace which has no pilot light will pay for itself in fuel economy alone in its first six years of operation.

In the past, life cycle costs have centered around the total use costs involved with the product. When the cost of fuel, maintenance, insurance, repair or replacement of parts and the like was added to the initial cost of a vehicle, the total cost became apparent. From these data, estimates could be made concerning the purchase of future cars. As an example, many people trade autos every two years, because they know that this is the time period that optimizes their life cycle costs. Of course, they don't use the same terms we use here in their thinking, but the effect is the same. In all probability, this two-year life cycle optimization was a strategy thought up on a slack day by an ambitious car salesman with a fair knowledge of life cycle costs! An interesting sidelight to the two-year cycle is the person who trades his two-year-old car because, "It is beginning to nickel and dime me to the poor house!"

More up to date, life cycle costs have taken a new quality/ reliability twist. For instance, a taxi cab company about to invest in an addition of 40 new cabs to its fleet, might make a statement such as this to the auto dealership: "We are willing to buy 40 autos from you according to the terms and conditions to which we have both agreed, except we wish to add the following stipulation":

> *Your estimate of fuel consumption for this auto is 24 miles per gallon. At the end of each fiscal quarter, we will tabulate the average fuel consumption for the average auto and we will total the fuel consumption for all 40 autos. Should our average fuel consumption for any month exceed expectations based on achieving a minimum of 19 miles per gallon for each cab, we will expect your company to pay for half of all excess fuel consumed. This stipulation will continue for four years even in the event that title to any or all autos is transferred to another owner.*

Another example of applied life cycle cost principles is the savings and loan company about to enter into a contract to buy 5,000 personal computers. The savings and loan company wants to add the following stipulation to the contract:

> *The computer is made up of five printed circuit board assemblies, one power supply, two disk drives, and a monitor. We intend to maintain these units ourselves. Should any of the component parts have more than 2 percent failures in any one month or more than 1 percent failures in any consecutive 12 months, you will redesign that assembly. In addition to furnishing the new design on all future shipments, you will furnish kits or exchange component parts to retrofit all computer workstations already installed in our field offices. This clause will be in effect for the life of the contract plus four years.*

Many useful calculations and estimates can be made with regard to the total (life cycle) cost of the product. As a matter of fact, life cycle costs are one measure of quality. Indeed in most cases, life cycle cost information can be used for quality improvement. Yet, this discussion of life cycle costs is presented mainly to avoid confusion with the analysis of the operating costs of quality that will be presented throughout the balance of this text.

Summary of Principles
1. Better quality is *not* more expensive.
2. Good quality is cheaper.
3. Good quality means increased productivity.

4. Good quality means higher profits. The idea of reducing the cost of quality to make profits soar is the basic premise for starting a cost of quality program.

5. In capsule form, there are four quality costs. Appendix A is made up of worksheets for each of the four quality costs—this appendix can also be used as a summary of the quality cost elements:

 a. Appraisal Cost — cost of inspection and test

 b. Prevention Cost — quality salaries and training

 c. Internal Failure Cost — scrap, rework and the like

 d. External Failure Cost — warranty and field failures

6. More luxurious designs *do* cost more, but this should not be confused with "operating quality costs."

7. Our analysis assumes the "fitness for use" of our design.

8. We want to assure "conformance to design."

9. Life cycle costs add up the total costs for using the item.

10. Total life costs are valid for comparison and trade-offs.

11. Life cycle costing is seldom used for quality improvement in the short run, although more and more it is being used as a "learning tool," especially in terms of improvement for the next generation of design.

NOTE: Throughout this book, the terms *cost of quality* and *quality costs* are used interchangeably.

CHAPTER 2

The Quality Cost Procedure

Collecting Quality Costs: Easy

Before we can start collecting quality costs, we should all be speaking the same language. Since one of the best reasons for establishing a procedure is to assure uniformity in our dealings with a subject, the following chapter discusses the cost of quality procedure in detail and should serve as a handy guide for writing your own procedure.

A sample cost of quality procedure has also been provided in Appendix B. You will note that while this procedure may not fit your organization exactly, it is complete in the sense that you can use it as an outline for writing your own procedure.

Contents of Quality Cost Procedure

In general the cost of quality procedure should look no different than the other operating procedures used by your company. Format and structure should conform, more or less, to the procedural style already in effect. Most often company procedures contain the following sections and related information:

- Scope: This outlines the specific plants, divisions, departments or sections where the procedure is to be in effect.
- Purpose: This tells what the procedure is intended for.
- Reference: These are the government, industry or company documents referenced in the procedure.
- Definitions: This is a glossary of terms and acronyms.
- General Requirements: This tells *what* is to be done.
- Detailed Procedure: This tells *how, what* is to be done.

How much information or detail should be included in each of these sections depends on company policy, size and structure. It may also depend upon who is expected to carry the burden of data collection and analysis, and the level of experience available in the personnel with the primary responsibility for performing the various tasks. As a general rule, smaller companies are usually more localized with regard to responsibilities. Thus, the procedure is much less detailed. In larger companies, with many more people involved in data collection and analysis, the procedure needs to be much more rigorous in order to assure the consistency and accuracy of the reported information.

As already noted, the level of detail depends on your company's operating environment. However, as a minimum, you must provide sufficient detail to allow understanding and repeatability of the process. In the following paragraphs we have described the basic contents of each section. As you go about writing your procedure, you may want to refer frequently to these paragraphs and determine the level of detail needed—when in doubt, provide more, not less detail.

Statement of Scope

The Scope section should describe what areas and/or aspects of company operations are likely to be influenced by the procedure. In most cases all areas within the company will participate, but in some companies only manufacturing divisions will be affected, while sales and leasing divisions may not. It is conceivable that different products or projects might require separate procedures to appropriately define data collection and reporting requirements.

Statement of Purpose

The Purpose section should concisely state the reason or intent of the procedure. The statement of purpose may take many forms, and the actual form you choose is up to you. For instance, the stated purpose of the procedure could be "to establish a common basis for interpretation of quality cost data," or "to establish the basic requirements for collection, analysis and reporting of quality cost data." Either statement of purpose is acceptable even though they are quite different in intent.

Referencing Related Documents

The Reference section normally contains a list of other company documents that are in some way relevant to the quality cost procedure. For example, the company's chart of accounts containing specific charge codes for each category of quality cost would be listed in this section. A reference might also be made to a contract number, if this procedure is the result of a contractual obligation to a specific customer, etc.

Definition of Terms

The Definition section of the procedure should include definitions of the quality cost categories as well as each of the specific subcategories. If a separate chart of quality cost accounts is going to be attached to the quality cost procedure, then definitions for specific subcategories may be omitted. However, as a minimum, all quality cost procedures should have definitions for general quality costs and major cost categories, i.e., prevention, appraisal, internal and external failure costs. See Chapter 3, Categories of Quality Costs, for detailed definitions.

Establish General Requirements

The General Requirements section should be used to describe general departmental responsibilities and requirements pertinent to collecting, analyzing and reporting quality cost data. It is also where the basic requirements are established for allocating overhead, what accounting reports are to be used, how cost estimates are to be handled, frequency of reports, etc. In other words, this section tells *what* will be done.

Detailed Procedure

This section of the quality cost Procedure is the place to establish *how, who* does *what* and *when.* Detailed instructions are given when necessary to ensure that tasks and calculations are consistently performed in the same manner. Report formats and distribution lists are established, and other specific requirements are detailed.

Remember, however, that the level of detail to be included in your quality cost procedure is up to you and must be appropriate to your company's operating environment. Be sure to include sufficient information to assure reliable,* repeatable results, but do not create a 20-page procedure if a five-page procedure is adequate.

Summary of Principles

1. Properly written procedures provide a sound basis for uniform dealing with a subject.

2. The basic elements and structure of a good cost of quality procedure will include the following:
   a. Scope
   b. Purpose
   c. Reference
   d. Definitions
   e. General Requirements
   f. Detailed Procedure

3. Procedures must be sufficiently detailed to assure understanding and repeatability of the intended result.

---

*Eighty-five percent accuracy done the same way for each accounting period is adequate initially, but this should quickly become 90 percent, then 95 percent accurate even before the system is completely entrusted to the computer (i.e., theoretical 100 percent accuracy).

CHAPTER 3

Categories of Quality Costs

The Rules about Quality Cost Categories

This chapter deals entirely with defining quality costs. A good understanding of quality costs is imperative before attempting to establish a quality cost program in any company. As you will find when you begin the process of collecting and analyzing data, "things aren't always as they appear to be." This is particularly true in the fast-paced, fluctuating industrial world of today. You must quickly develop a feel for what is, or is not, a legitimate quality cost. You must also learn to consistently sort costs for analysis and make valid judgments about their avoidability.

General Quality Costs

In general, quality costs are defined as:

... all expenses which are incurred in the assurance and control of the manufacture of products which meet the customer's requirements. In other words, the cost of quality could be visualized as those expenses which would not exist if we were able to design and build products that were totally free of defects.

Prevention Costs

Any money spent for minimizing failure and appraisal costs falls into the prevention cost category. Generally, quality planning, data collection, analysis and reporting and such are included. No matter who does the work, the cost of any of the tasks below are listed under prevention:

Planning: Cost of development of quality policy, preparation of the quality plan and inspection procedures, establishment of standards, the operation of training programs and any like activities. Planning costs are often hidden by farming work out to another function and letting the charges for the work accrue to that function. As an example, when an inspector is called upon to outline an inspection procedure, the time used should be charged to prevention. However, such work is usually included in the inspector's time that is charged to appraisal.

Test Engineering: Cost of test equipment and the development of procedures and software needed for continued product conformance. No matter if this type of work is done by the design engineers or the test technicians, it still is test engineering.

Reliability Engineering: Cost of new product evaluation, parts, materials and process qualifications as well as reliability analyses, maintainability studies and failure analyses. Often, parts, material and process work done by component engineers is lost in payroll accounting when it should be included in this subcategory.

Quality Information Systems: Costs associated with the collection, "crunching" and reporting of all forms of data related to quality. Quality information costs are sometimes mischarged to the computer group when the hours for this type of computer work are not translated to the quality cost file.

Appraisal Costs

Generally, these costs have to do with determining the acceptability of the product as it is being made. Included are first-time inspection and testing, calibration expense and audit activities. First-time inspection and test is emphasized, since screening of a failed lot, retesting of a reworked assembly or reinspection of repaired product are all the result of a failure and thus are properly listed under the failure cost category.

Inspection: Cost of verifying conformance to specification of all parts, materials and processes. Usually, this includes incoming inspection, in-process inspection, final acceptance and all auditing. Reinspection and retest as a result of engineering changes, which is really a cost due to failure, is often mischarged to this category.

Production Test: This is the cost of all of the areas included under inspection, except that the verification of conformance involves testing rather than inspection. Life testing, or other reliability testing falls into a gray area. It may require a case-by-case evaluation for the decision to move this cost into the prevention area. The important thing is that like cases are always put in the same category.

Calibration and Maintenance: This includes the cost of all calibration contracts, laboratory expenses, maintenance and repair associated with the operation of the calibration system. Lost time and retesting because of out-of-calibration problems are correctly charged to this subcategory.

Quality Audit: All of the costs associated with the evaluation of the effectiveness of procedures, equipment and methods as well as periodic evaluations of the product's ability to meet customers' needs are included here. When a periodic audit is substituted for acceptance testing, costs are correctly listed under inspection.

Failure Costs

These are the costs which are brought on by deficiencies of design, parts, materials or processes. Failure costs are usually separated into internal and external failures.

The specific causes of failure costs listed below will not be segregated since some of the costs, such as material review board, could accrue to internal or external. However, it is important to list failure costs in the right category since ratios are important tools for optimization of the product's overall quality cost.

Rework or Repair: Any cost resulting from deficiencies of parts, materials, processes, workmanship or design. This includes anything that is needed to bring any nonconforming product to the state that it will perform its function in the intended manner. It is well to remember that rework is defined as bringing the product to blueprint configuration. Repair means that the repaired part does not conform to the blueprint, but will perform all required functions. These costs are often circumvented by making unauthorized repairs. Each time a worker files the edge of a printed circuit board to make it fit, and continues to charge his time to the make work order, your repair costs lose some accuracy.

Inspection of Rework: All cost of reinspections due to repair or rework activities, including rework resulting from design changes and engineering orders. This can be a two-way street—sometimes an inspection supervisor will camouflage his appraisal costs by having his inspectors charge the cost to a current engineering change order.

Testing of Rework: In addition to the cost of retest, any time used in isolating causes or readjusting the product are to be included.

Material Review Actions: Costs associated with processing, evaluation of, or disposition of discrepant materials are to be included. This includes the cost of scrap, replacement of material, internal and external rework charges as well as the standard paperwork cost for processing an action by the material review board. Review and approval tasks by engineering, purchasing, marketing and others are sometimes missed when this subcategory is tabulated.

Warranty Costs: All costs attendant to repair, service or replacement of product under warranty. This includes monies budgeted against future warranty expenses. Misguided marketing people will sometimes extend the guarantee for favorite customers. Or they will ship gratis replacement parts for out-of-date assemblies. These are correctly advertising or good will costs. They are not quality costs at all.

Returned Material: This applies to costs of material returned without replacement by customers. This cost usually includes the loss of the "if sold" income value, but it may also consider the loss of good will and loss of future sales factors.

Complaint Adjustment: All costs of investigation and adjustment of complaints stemming from deficiencies of product or installation of product. (When the complaint is not justified, this cost should be charged to marketing [good will or advertising] instead of quality.)

Discounts or Allowances: Any concession given to a customer in return for accepting substandard product. This includes a reduced price (discount) in return for a "use as is" disposition by the customer and any loss of income due to dumping or the sale of down-graded products as seconds or irregulars. Ten percent off of last year's model would be listed in this file.

Avoidable Costs

No discussion of quality costs is complete without offering some consideration of avoidable costs, or avoidable quality costs. For our purposes the following definition of avoidable costs will serve as the intended meaning whenever this term is used in subsequent sections within this text:*

A cost may be considered avoidable whenever it can be eliminated, or significantly reduced, by a corrective action that costs less to implement and maintain than would a continuance of the preexisting condition over a specified period of time.

Summary of Principles

1. By definition, quality costs are those costs which would go away if we could design and build our product right every time.

2. Quality cost categories and subcategories are:

Prevention Costs
      Planning
      Test Engineering
      Reliability Engineering
      Quality Information Systems
Appraisal Costs
      Inspection
      Production Test
      Calibration and Maintenance
      Quality Audit

*For additional details on avoidable costs and costs of quality see *The Quality Control Handbook,* Third Edition, J.M. Juran.

Failure Costs†
> Rework or Repair
> Inspection of Rework
> Testing of Rework
> Material Review Actions
> Warranty Costs
> Returned Material
> Complaint Adjustment
> Discounts or Allowances

3. Avoidable quality costs are those costs that can be cost-effectively reduced or eliminated.

---

†Those which occur before shipment are called internal failure costs—after shipment they are external failure costs.

CHAPTER 4

Collection of Quality Costs Data

Bringing Costs into the Open

The short-term manager might try to circumvent an efficient quality cost program. Nothing threatens this misguided manager (in his own mind) more than an accurate listing of failure costs. Since most of us are muddled or misled by similar emotions, it is important to know the answer to: "Who will look better if scrap and failure costs are hidden or minimized?" When you determine who has a vested interest, you are on your way to finding the answers to: "How do they hide it?" and "How can I bring it out in the open?" These answers are not easy to find and you must be a diplomat. Yet, you must know the answers if you are going to be able to bring these costs into the open so they may be dealt with.

When the cost of quality program is in its final form, the accounting department should have the responsibility for collecting the data and reporting trends to management. When this becomes a reality, it will be the quality department's responsibility to provide the analysis for interim fluctuations and to recommend the actions required to maximize profits by reducing the costs of quality.

Initially, the gathering of quality cost data must be the responsibility of the quality department. When you show management the great increase in profits that can be gained through reasonably accurate quality cost figures, you will have the impetus for a fully integrated reporting system. The sources and methods outlined here will yield immediate quality cost information that may be used to get your system under way. (The quality cost account structure presented in Appendix C provides a good check list for the determination of a charge sorting system.)

Getting the Data

There are a number of accounting reports that will be quite useful in your effort to gather cost of quality data. However, you must be careful to evaluate the data in these reports. As previously stated, the accountant's definition for terms such as scrap and rework is different from those which are commonly used by production people. You need to review their data, and when necessary reallocate it to the proper cost categories. If you are thorough and consistent, the corrected data will be an accurate reflection of actual quality costs.

General Ledger: In theory, all of the figures that you will ever need are in the general ledger. In actual fact, this may be true, but you can't find them. For instance, intangibles such as loss of good will or poor customer satisfaction are rarely listed. Other quality costs are often hidden in material and labor costs, and scrap costs are often mixed into the operating costs. Usable data from the general ledger needs to be evaluated and in most cases, you will need one of the accountants to guide you in your search.

Operating Statement: This is another rich data source, but the same cautions for use apply as those for the general ledger. The operating statement is the best source for revenue information. When quality costs are graphed as a percentage of revenue, fluctuating monthly data is somewhat "smoothed." (Most manufacturing calendars have two 4-week months and one 5-week month each quarter.)

Labor Distribution: The labor distribution figures can also be used as a base for smoothing the graphs of the various quality cost categories. Rework and repair costs (including reinspection and retest) hidden in these figures can usually be estimated by percentage and then moved to the correct categories.

Estimating Quality Costs

After determining what costs are really costs of quality, it may take a little mathematical reasoning to establish the correct amounts that belong in each category.

One early estimate (rough but effective) is to make a fairly complete study of the costs of items that are returned in one month. Using this figure as your total failure cost, you can estimate your total cost of quality for the month as twice the amount. It is not unusual to find that this first estimate turns out to be about 25 percent of your company's total revenue.

The following areas are good sources of information for your estimates of quality costs:

Supervisor or Line Engineer: The area supervisor or the engineer responsible for the line usually has an excellent knowledge of how the hours are being used. In the manufacturing areas, these people will usually have records to show what jobs were done and about how many hours were used on each. Often, rework and repair jobs are already identified. If not, these are the best people to estimate percentages of time lost to the quality cost categories. These estimates should be accurate to within 2 percent of actual. These same people can usually tell you their standard costs almost to the penny—i.e., the allocated hours and material for their production area—which will help you in identifying losses to accrue to the cost of quality.

Percentage Allocation of Hours or Dollars: Sometimes it is necessary to estimate quality costs by taking percentages of the total. With a little investigation (audit) you can estimate the portion of the total operating costs that should be allocated to the cost of quality categories. This will probably be different for material than for payroll hours. It will certainly differ by department. However, if one is reasonably prudent in the estimation process, the cost of quality allocations should be at least as accurate as plus or minus 10 percent.

Development of Standards: When there are only incomplete records, and no one to estimate, and standards haven't been established, you will have to develop your own. To do this, you need to estimate the cost of the material and the cost of labor needed to make a good part. You may even have to estimate the payroll and the material used by production. By subtracting one from the other you will get quality cost estimates that should be close enough to alert management to the fact that your company can triple its profit by better record keeping and intelligent follow-up in the quality cost area.

Using Actual Quality Costs

We know that a system based on actual costs will give the most accurate cost of quality information. But any accounting system depends on the discipline of inputs; and quality cost systems can be thwarted and the costs of quality can be camouflaged by on-purpose misdirection of work order reporting and returned material allowances.

Labor Distribution and Material Control: Most organizations have a work order system for time card accounting already in place. Usually, some of the numbers of the work order can be allocated for quality cost accounting. If not, cost codes can be added as a suffix to the work order number. The cost account structures presented in Appendices B and C use three digits. With such a system, discipline is enhanced by the supervisor's ability to recognize the various quality cost categories by the first two digits of the code and computer sorting becomes easy. Similarly, the material accounting could be coded according to "first-time manufacture" or "required for rework" and the like which would make a software solution to sorting and feedback easy.

Accounting Reports: Once the accounting system is in place, almost all of the tabulation will come from routine accounting data. Accounting will be responsible for the charting of quality data and the quality department will interpret the trends and direct and coordinate profit improvement efforts.

Field data will usually require external inputs. This too can be machine tabulated, by using accounts codes as shown and appropriate software.

Allocation of Overhead

Once you have done the work necessary to assemble the cost of quality data from the various accounting reports and estimates, you will need to add the overhead expenses associated with these costs. Simply stated, overhead is the cost of activities, facilities, benefits and the like that are required to support the actual production and delivery of the company's product or service.

Consider, for example, the production worker on a typical assembly line. The required overhead to support his assembly activities includes expenses for benefits (such as health insurance, vacation and holidays), rent for the space he and his workbench occupy, cost of his equipment and costs associated with supervision, production scheduling, industrial engineering, etc. All these expenses, and many more, are part of the overhead expense or burden that must be applied to his labor.

Overhead costs, then, are said to burden direct labor and material expenses, and consequently the burden rate is the ratio of overhead required to support various direct labor and material expenses.

There are two basic ways in which overhead costs can be determined. The first is to approach your accounting department and request from them a burden rate estimate that can be used as a multiplier of direct labor and material expenses. In general, your accountant will give a number such as 2.0, 2.5 or the like, which he feels is sufficient for the intended purpose. In some cases, he will give separate burden rates for labor and material.

The second way, which is far more difficult, is to calculate the actual (or a close approximation) of the burden rate from accounting data. To do this requires an intricate knowledge of organizational structures and a willingness to devote the hours needed to compile the data. A sample of what a burden rate calculation might look like is contained in Figure 3. As you will note, percent allocations from various supporting departments have been made to load the appropriate expenses into the test department's burden rate. Determining the burden rate in this fashion will result in establishing different burden rates for almost every cost of quality subcategory. If you wish to use this method of calculating burden rates, you can develop worksheets for your company based on the sample worksheet shown in Figure 3.

While using an accountant's estimate to establish the burden rate(s) is probably acceptable, the second method shown here is more precise. It may result in significantly different data from the first on a category-by-category basis. However, assuming an enlightened accounting department there should be little difference in the overall figures.

Test:

Indirect Labor Salaries $14,768
@ 100% of Final Test (Dept. 440) salaries.

Overhead Expenses $52,271
@ 100% of Final Test (Dept. 440)
operating expenses $25,414

Plus 50% of Manufacturing Administration (Dept. 420)
salary and operating expenses and
associated operations (Dept. 401)
allocations. . . . . $ 4,646

Plus 25.7% of operations (Dept. 401)
salary and operating expenses $22,211

Total Indirect and Overhead Expenses $67,039

Burden Rate (Total Costs/Indirect Costs = 67,039/14,768 = 4.54

Figure 3 — Overhead Worksheet

A burden rate of 4.54 means that for estimating or budgeting purposes an hour of an employee's time at a pay rate of $10.00 per hour must equal $45.40 per hour with overhead included (i.e., Pay Rate × Burden Rate = $10.00 × 4.54).

Now, in determining the burden rate you may choose either of two (2) approaches: If you wish to use burden rate as an adder, then simply divide the Overhead Expenses figure by the Indirect Labor Salaries figure and the resulting ratio will represent the amount that must be added to the basic category cost to adjust for overhead (in this case 3.54). On the other hand, should you wish to use the burden rate as a multiplier, you must add 1.0 to the ratio to account for the basic category expense in the computation, i.e., your burden rate in this case will be 4.54.

Summary of Principles

1. To get the program started, the quality department must assume all responsibility in connection with the cost of quality effort.

2. When the cost of quality program is mature, the accounting department will have the responsibility for collecting data and reporting quality costs to management. The quality department will provide the analyses and direct the profit improvement efforts.

3. Sources for quality costs may come from:
   - accounting
   - area supervisors
   - percentage allocations
   - audits
   - labor distributions
   - material control
   - and estimates of any or all of these

4. Collection and analysis of quality cost data should lead to profit improvement by finding and eliminating the sources of the quality costs. Doubling company profits should be commonplace for most companies. Increasing profit three-fold or more would not be unusual.

CHAPTER 5

Analysis of Quality Costs

Introduction

A company may be just starting its cost of quality program or it may already have a formal accounting system in place, but the following items need to be followed: quality cost data should be tabulated according to the categories and subcategories outlined in Chapter 3, and according to the guidelines listed here and in Chapter 4. Overhead has been mentioned as a quality cost contributor; thus departments that generate an appreciable amount of quality costs should be allocated some portion of the overhead as an add-on. Lastly, should the quality costs be graphed by accountants or by the quality department? It remains for the quality people to be the leaders in making the analysis. Soon, supervision and upper management will realize the power of quality cost tabulation toward improvement of profit and they will join in and begin to make their own analyses.

Compiling the Data

The major tool for the analysis of quality cost information is a tabulation of each of the subcategories for comparison. The tabular presentation of quality cost information makes it easy to spot trends. When this data is graphed, it is a great sales tool: first you can use the graph to attract management attention and support by demonstrating potential profit improvements. You can continue to get support by demonstrating how the quality costs go away during the corrective action and control phases. Everyone wants to go with a winner.

Once we have identified the quality costs that can be avoided, we must ask "Where should we start?" Often there is so much room for improvement that the quality engineer says, "Start anywhere! It's just like cutting grass when it is tall—anyplace you mow, the improvement is seen immediately!" While it is true that anything you do will show improvement, it is still better to look around to find those areas where the most improvement can be made with the least amount of effort. The Pareto analysis is the best way to do this.

Simplified, the Pareto analysis starts with a listing of all the elements of a study in descending order. As a general rule, the first 15 percent of the entries will contain 85 percent of the total. This means that by the time you identify the three most expensive factors of a quality cost element, they will contain the bulk of the costs of the entire element.

The following is a brief example of how a Pareto analysis works:

Category:	Internal Failure Cost	$176,832
Element:	Engineering Change Order (ECO) Rework	$ 99,755
Factors	Memory Board (MEMB)	$ 44,700
of ECO	Mother Board (MOTB)	$ 31,252
Rework:	Power Supply (PWRS)	$ 14,270
	All Others (ALLO)	$ 9,533
	Total of Factors	$ 99,755

From this simple analysis it becomes obvious that the most fruitful areas for improvement are the Memory Board, the Mother Board, and the Power Supply. It still remains to be determined where these avoidable costs are coming from and how to reduce them, but the knowledge that we have 45 percent of the total (25 percent of the whole category) to attack in the Memory Board alone is an excellent starting point.

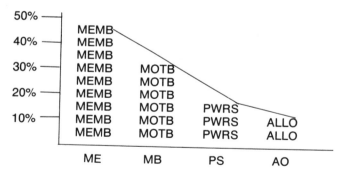

Figure 4 — Pareto Analysis 1
(Factors shown as % of the element cost)

A Pareto analysis can be graphed in many forms and in any media—these are shown in typed figures to illustrate computer or word processor capability. Another illustration of the data from the previous example is shown in Figure 5. When this type chart is shown on an overhead viewgraph one week, and the next week's viewgraph (shown in Figure 6) uses the same dollar scale, the second can be laid on top of the first for a graphic display of improvement.

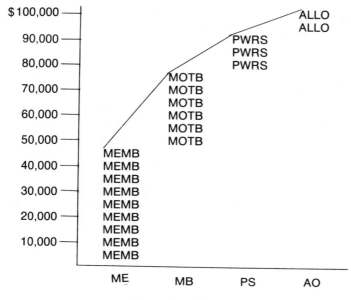

Figure 5 — Week One

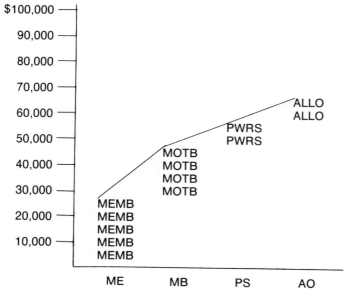

Figure 6 — Week Two

Now let's go through another Pareto example to be sure that we really understand the basic principle.

Category:	Failure Cost		$176,832
Element:	Test Debug and Rework		$ 70,994
Factors	Power Supply (PWRS)	$ 31,947	
of Rework:	Input-Output Board (IOBD)	$ 21,298	
	Mother Board (MOTB)	$ 14,199	
	All Others (ALLO)	$ 3,550	
	Total of Factors	$ 70,994	

Here, it is obvious that the Power Supply offers the greatest savings opportunity, at 50 percent of the total for the element and 20 percent of the total for the category.

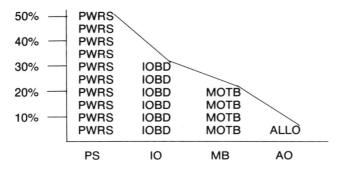

Figure 7 — Pareto Analysis 2
(Factors shown as % of the element cost)

Workmanship	Components
1. Wiring Error	9. Mistuned
2. Short (actual or potential)	10. Strapping Error
3. Wrong Polarity	11. Semiconductor
4. Missing Component	12. Resistor
5. Damaged Component	13. Capacitor
6. Wrong Value Component	14. Inductor
7. Improper Soldering	15. Transformer-Filter-Relay
8. All Others	16. Lamp Switch

Figure 8 — Defect Descriptions (and Code Numbers)

Another way to display quality costs for effective analysis is to display them as a matrix. In the figure below, the defect descriptions are in code numbers across the top and the assemblies are in a column on the left. The numbers inside the matrix show how many times the defect appeared in the assembly at the end of the line.

This matrix allows one to Pareto-ize by assembly (see numbers behind each assembly name) and by type of defect.

ASSEMBLY	1	2	3	4	5	6	7	8	9	10	11	12	13	14	15	16
Mother Board (44)		9		15	6	3		11								
Power Supply (28)							2	2				6			18	
Memory Board (22)	7		3			9		3								
All Others (14)	1	3	1	2	2	1	1	3								
Total (108)	8	12	4	17	8	13	3	19				6			18	

Figure 9 — Matrix
(All amounts shown are in frequency of occurrence)

One must look at all factors when analyzing quality costs. As an example, the matrix from the last section is evaluated in this example, according to the costs of the defects involved. Each defect has a cost assigned to it. The numbers of defects are the same as in the last example but now the numbers inside the matrix are cost figures in dollars.

1. Wiring Error	$10		9. Mistuned	$1
2. Short (actual or potential)	$1		10. Strapping Error	$1
3. Wrong Polarity	$1		11. Semiconductor	$1
4. Missing Component	$1		12. Resistor	$1
5. Damaged Component	$1		13. Capacitor	$1
6. Wrong Value Component	$8		14. Inductor	$1
7. Improper Soldering	$1		15. Transformer-Fltr-Relay	$5
8. All Others	$1		16. Lamp Switch	$1

Figure 10 — Defect Descriptions (Codes and Costs included)

ASSEMBLY	1	2	3	4	5	6	7	8	9	10	11	12	13	14	15	16
Mother Board (65)		9		15	6	24		11								
Power Supply (100)							2	2				6			90	
Memory Board (148)	70		3			72		3								
All Others (30)	10	3	1	2	2	8	1	3								
Total (343)	80	12	4	17	8	104	3	19				6			90	

Figure 11 — Matrix
(All amounts shown are in dollars)

It is easy to see that the dollar amounts establish other priorities than were called for when the matrix figures were simply defects.

Index for Quality Costs

Many bases can be used to index quality costs. Those listed below are not intended to be all inclusive. Some bases may be specialized— used only for a certain type of industry, hence left off this list. If you want to use an index, not listed here, which fits your purposes better, feel free to do so!

- Total revenue
- Cost of manufacturing
- Cost of sales
- Standard manufacturing costs
- Costs of productive labor
- Total sales volume
- Process costs (especially applicable to an added value operation)

One index that should *never* be used for normalizing quality costs is net profit. Net profit can vary as the result of many factors. Use of net profit as a basis for comparison will usually result in many extraneous agitations, making analysis virtually impossible.

One last note of advice: It is best to use two or more bases for comparison. Using only one base for comparison often leaves the process without the crosscheck needed to prevent the data from sending us on an occasional wild goose chase.

Calculations need to be made before the data is graphed. Usually the decision as to which of the indices will be used as the base for the display narrows down to one of the following:

- Sales revenue
- Manufacturing costs
- Sales costs

Other indices may be used although sales revenues seem to be chosen most often. In the usual case, each of the four major categories of quality costs for the reporting period is divided by the sales revenue for that same period.

Sometimes the manufacturing costs, which are used as the index, are for a previous period to match the lag in the reporting of the cost data. No matter what the index used, it is important that it be used every month in order to give the same basis for comparison.

Once you have selected your index for charting quality costs, you are ready to begin graphing the data if you wish. However, it is best that you first apply a smoothing technique to the data prior to graphing. The most common method for doing this is the use of a three-month rolling average. The data for the current period is added to the data for the previous two periods and divided by three. When these data are displayed, most perturbations (large or erratic points on the graph) are smoothed and the general trend is easier to spot. This three-month rolling average method has the added feature of always using the data for the two 4-week months and the one 5-week month, which most manufacturing companies use. (NOTE: This 5-week month feature is already somewhat smoothed by use of the indices, especially sales revenues.)

Analysis of Costs

Ratios between the categories of quality cost vary according to the kind of industry. Indeed, quality cost category ratios are usually held as private company data. Thus, many industries develop their own ratios, based on empirical data. When you are first starting, and the ratio for your industry or company isn't known, a good guideline is that the total for both failure cost categories be 50 percent of the grand total. There are a couple of subguidelines—that the failure costs should be about a ratio of 1 to 9, internal to external—and a ratio of 1 to 4 for prevention costs versus appraisal costs. However, the most important criterion to strive for is a beneficial trend of the total cost of quality line. In other words, a detectable and continuous decrease in the overall cost of quality as a percentage of revenue.

Important to quality cost analysis are the fluctuations of the costs in the subcategories. A small change between categories may well be the result of a large change in a subcategory. And this information may be the clue that leads to reasons for the increase.

As in all chart analyses, one should be looking for assignable causes. Several items might be listed as probables, and identification of the most often occurring, or the most probable (i.e., Pareto-izing) leads to the next step.

When the probable causes are assessed, a plan to remedy the situation or to bring about corrective action is needed. This is best done by the action item method, wherein the person or persons with the greatest expertise in the area are assigned to investigate and correct. Meeting on a regular basis to report progress usually brings about the most profit improvement. This and other methods for implementing corrective actions will be discussed in detail in Chapter 7.

Considerations for Comparison

In the ideal situation, we could take our table of quality costs and compare it to a composite of all of the quality costs collected from companies that are in the same business. Unfortunately, there are no industry standards to relate to. Even if you have worked for other companies similar to your own, the diversity of reporting methods and the uncertainties of management give a low confidence level in using past experience as a comparison standard.

Standards for quality cost comparison are often given in a general way. One corporate quality director for a large manufacturing company conducted training classes for quality managers from several of the company's divisions. One of the facts that was presented in these seminars was:

"Our quality costs are running right at 6 percent!"

This was followed by:

"While this is better than industry standards, your major effort in this area is to bring your cost of quality down to 4 percent."

This cost of quality training program was a success, based on the number of divisions in this company which started reporting these costs. Unfortunately, once the division quality manager had his quality cost reporting system in place, he found no basis for the 6 percent industry standard and that meeting the 4 percent figure was impossible. The corporate quality manager would have done better to tell the division managers to keep records to monitor division performance—and then develop an improvement program.

Incidentally, the corporate quality manager didn't mention the base to be used for either of these figures. Most of the division quality managers assumed that the index to be used was the division's revenue figure, and used it as the only base.

In general, there seems to be a feeling in American industry that an actual cost of quality, (as a percent of sales) optimizes at 2.5 percent. There is a rumor that this figure is less than 1 percent in Japan. Neither of these figures are completely valid, but if they were, comparison of your own first estimates to either of these optimums would probably bring such frustration that you would be tempted to shelve the whole program. It is interesting to note that according to this same rumor, the Japanese 1 percent subscribes to the same optimum ratios between categories as the American 2.5 percent.

Faced with an insurmountable task such as the 4 percent goal, the quality manager could be tempted to bury some of the avoidable costs of quality in the standard costs. This should not be done.

It is better for the new cost of quality program to face the fact that there are no industry standards for comparison. This means that your best comparisons will relate to past history and current trends. Graphing quality costs by category will show trends as well as the relationship between them. One needs to know how to interpret the changes and to be able to identify seasonal, or one-time variations for earlier trend interpretations.

Normal trends to be noted in the quality cost categories at different points in the development of a quality cost program are listed below. These trend descriptions offer a fairly valid standard to check against, not because they are written in stone, but rather that they are, more or less, the standards which identify the different phases of the program.

At the beginning of the cost of quality reporting, all of the quality costs will show a rising trend. This is as much due to the refinements of collecting the data as it is to the added activity.

When your cost of quality program is working—i.e., you have been able to identify some of the major avoidable costs and have had some success in avoiding them—the failure costs and the appraisal costs will go down.

Finally, all quality cost categories will begin to go down as program control is established. Some experts believe that the cost of quality will eventually reach a plateau, which is then the optimum. Other experts think the beneficial trend will continue until all of the avoidable costs have been eliminated.

Summary of Principles

1. Pareto analyses and matrices are useful tools for choosing those quality cost factors which offer the most return for effort expended in searching out avoidable costs.

2. Some of the bases that may be used for equalizing quality cost figures are listed here:
   - Total revenue
   - Cost of manufacturing
   - Cost of sales
   - Standard manufacturing costs
   - Costs of productive labor
   - Total sales volume
   - Process costs

3. Net profit should never be used as an index for quality costs.

4. It is best to index against two or more bases for comparison.

5. Most often, quality cost data is graphed as a percentage of:
   - Sales revenue
   - Manufacturing costs
   - Sales costs

6. Quality cost graphs may be presented as a rolling average to smooth out fluctuations.

7. Quality costs may be analyzed according to the relationships of

the various categories or against the company's history.

8. Collection and analysis of quality cost data will lead to higher profits by finding and eliminating the sources of the quality costs.

9. There are no absolute industry standards for quality costs.

10. For historical comparisons the following are generally true:

- All quality costs seem to be higher in the beginning of any quality cost program.

- Failure costs and appraisal cost go down once the quality cost program is working.

- All quality cost categories will go down when the quality costs are under control.

CHAPTER 6

The Cost of Quality Report

Introduction

Once the fundamental system for collecting and analyzing the costs associated with quality has been established, it is time to prepare your first management report to begin your campaign for soliciting support for improvement projects. This chapter includes a sample report and gives you suggestions for getting management approval to proceed on your profit improvement program.

You do not need to follow the format and recommendations given here exactly. These illustrations are provided to give you a general idea of where to start and how to proceed in going after the help you need to put your cost reduction program into action.

Report Formats

Your report format may be different from that used by any other company, but generally it should include some form of cover letter, a detailed cost summary and one or more trend charts. The following guidelines are offered:

- *Cover Letter:* Quality cost trends should be noted and improvement areas should be identified. A good distribution plan would be a monthly report with a review of the improvement program's progress included in the end-of-the-quarter letter.

- *Detailed Cost Summary:* Costs are best presented in tabular form with comments concerning short-term and long-term trends. Improvement suggestions should be included even when the trend line seems to be beneficial (i.e., how to make the trend even better).

- *Trend Charts:* These charts are the graphical presentation of the quality cost data. Trends are easy to spot on graphs and a chart showing beneficial trends is a great motivator for continuation and more effort toward the improvement project program.

Illustration of Cost of Quality Report

The quality cost report (Figure 13) is quite similar to an actual report prepared by the quality manager of a start-up company. This illustration is particularly appropriate because the quality manager used estimates and ingenuity to determine some of these costs.

Wherever possible, he based his figures on hard accounting data (about 60 percent of his total data). Since this was his first report to management, he was trying to impress the staff with the value of cost of quality reporting in the area of profit improvement. He reasoned that this was the best way to sell top management on the concept. Because this report is for a start-up company—i.e., a company that hasn't delivered product on a regular basis—internal and external failure costs have not been separated. This should not be a problem since the dividing line between internal and external failure costs is usually so well defined that tabulating the costs together should be of little consequence.

Prevention costs were based on the hourly rates of the personnel doing the work, multiplied by the quality manager's estimate of the hours used for prevention tasks. An accurate estimate of the data acquisition task was possible because this was the quality manager's own time. No cost is shown for the reliability task since this resource is to be added later. The burden rate was estimated using two factors: the first was an estimate of the cost of the service allocated to each of the charging functions by the overhead department; the second factor was based on actual figures covering vacations, sick time, health insurance, etc. and the fixed costs associated with the facility, as released by the accounting department. (For explanation of the burden rate, review pages 22-23).

Estimating appraisal costs was a matter of taking the payroll figures and estimating the split between first-time appraisal and the time spent on reinspection or debug (debug is the term used to describe the testing, analysis and repair of complex assemblies). Calibration services was a known figure since this job was contracted to an outside laboratory.

Estimate of the internal failure costs had a head start because of the division of work needed to separate the inspection and test jobs, and ECO rework, i.e., work due to engineering change orders, was well documented. (There was no assembly rework as such at this stage of development.) Material review board costs (MRB) were finally estimated at $3,066. This was the sum of $1,066 (the cost of material scrapped by material review action) and $50 each (for documentation costs) for the 40 MRB actions during May.

External failure costs were also easy since there was almost no product in the field, as this was a start-up company, and the $7,549 was an accounting allocation for warranty.

In his cover letter, the quality manager emphasized that the failure cost alone, i.e., $202,478, was almost 10 percent of the company's revenue. He also pointed out that, with hard work, the profit picture could be increased by 60 percent simply by reducing the total quality cost ($281,448) by 25 percent.

June 5, 19xx

TO: Chief Executive Officer

FROM: Quality Manager

SUBJECT: First Summary, Cost of Quality Analysis

In summary, the first Cost of Quality Analysis shows that our mistakes cost us:

$202,478 during the month of May

It also shows that it cost us:

$ 78,970 to find these mistakes.

We can improve our profit picture by:

$ 70,000 (60 percent improvement)

By investing in the effort to reduce our quality costs by 25 percent!

Copies:
Chief Engineer
Chief of Procurement
Manager Marketing
Manager Manufacturing
Manager Industrial Engineering
Chief Accountant

Figure 12 — Cover Letter to Management

MAY, 19xx
Revenues 2,108,588

Cost of Quality Category
as percent of

	Actual Expense	Burden Rate	Total Expense	Total Cost of Quality	Revenue	Cost of Sales	Cost of Mfg.
PREVENTION COSTS							
Q E Planning	5,192	2.49	12,928				
Test Engineering	14,616	2.11	30,840				
Reliability Eng.							
Data Acquis/Analysis	557	2.41	1,342				
Total Prevention Costs			45,110	16.0	2.1	5.1	12.9
APPRAISAL COSTS							
Inspection	7,805	2.33	18,186				
Production Test	2,222	4.00	8,888				
Calibration Serv.	1,805		1,805				
Quality Audit	1,961	2.54	4,981				
Total Appraisal Costs			33,860	12.0	1.6	3.8	9.7
FAILURE COSTS							
Internal Failure Costs							
Assembly Rework							
ECO Rework	29,651	3.66	108,523				
Inspection Rework	1,435	2.33	3,344				
Test Debug & Rework	19,999	4.00	79,996				
MRB	3,066		3,066				
Total Int Failure Costs			194,929				
External Failure Costs							
Complaint Adjustment							
Returned Material							
Warranty Charges	7,549		7,549				
Allowances							
Total Ext Failure Costs			7,549				
Total Failure Costs			202,478	72.0	9.6	22.8	57.8
TOTAL COST OF QUALITY:			281,448	100.00	13.3	31.7	80.4

Figure 13 — Detailed Cost Summary

NOTE: Quality Cost figures for March and April have been assembled,
but have only been used for the Trend Charts.

Straight Talk to Top Management

Everything that we have learned so far, in some part, helps us to determine how best to attract the attention of top management! The following list of rules is proposed as your guideline for getting and holding the attention of top management.

- You need to show an accurate picture of the costs of quality:
- — The magnitude of the cost must attract management attention;
- — The presentation of the costs should be simple;
- — All of the costs of quality should be summarized by category.
- The most fruitful areas should be identified:

r = % of Revenue
s = % of Sales
m = % of Manufacturing Costs

Percent

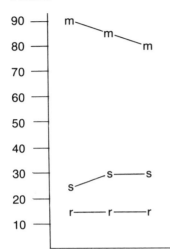

	MAR	APR	MAY
Revenues	2,086	1,988	2,109
Cost of Sales	966	857	888
Cost of Mfg.	292	328	350
Cost of Quality	270	276	281
Cost of Quality as Percent of:			
Revenue	13.0	13.9	13.3
Cost of Sales	28.0	32.2	31.7
Cost of Mfg.	92.6	84.2	80.4

Figure 14 — Total Cost of Quality (COQ) Category Trend Chart

NOTE: All dollar figures are in thousands.
All percentages shown are Total Cost of Quality divided by the Index shown.

— This may be shown by a Pareto analysis;
— Costs of quality may be presented in matrix form;
— Quality cost trends should be identified and analyzed.
• Potential savings as a result of reduction of quality cost areas can be presented:
— Profit improvements should be estimated;
— Expenditures for improvement must be evaluated and justified.
To get your message across you need to talk to top management. In other words, you need to convince top management that the costs of

p = Prevention Costs
a = Appraisal Costs
f = Failure Costs

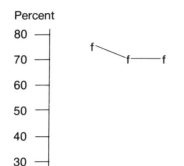

Percent

	MAR	APR	MAY
Prevention	15.6	16.3	16.0
Appraisal	9.8	10.7	12.0
Failure	74.6	73.0	72.0

Figure 15 — Major Cost of Quality (COQ) Category Trend Chart

NOTE: The figures shown are percentages, which were found
using the following formula:

Percent of Category = (COQ Category ÷ Total COQ) × 100

quality will make a significant difference to the profit structure and
that a serious improvement effort can eliminate them and thus is a
worthy investment. By pointing out the area where the most profit
improvement can be made with the least effort (Pareto presentation)
and justifying the expenditure of the effort by projecting the return on
investment, you will be able to get total commitment from your
management.

Once top management sees the profit improvement that results
from the control of quality costs, continuing analysis of the quality
cost trends will guide us to future savings and become the
measurement tool which demonstrates the overall worth of the
program.

In the following example, we will make a detailed analysis of one of the subcategories of the detailed cost summary presented in Figure 13. The subcategory to be analyzed is:

Test Debug and Rework $79,996

This single quality cost represents 39 percent of all of the failure costs and is 28 percent of the total quality costs. Indeed, because of these high percentages, this is considered to be a fertile area for savings.

A Pareto analysis of test debug and rework failure costs is shown below:

MWH923	$ 40,822
MWH930	19,586
MWH925	9,552
All Others	$ 10,036
Total	$ 79,996

NOTE: The model numbers are for specific printed circuit boards from model MWH, which are being tested.

All of the components on these printed circuit boards are integrated circuits (ICs). The $79,996 is the cost for finding and replacing 6,154 ICs, or about $13 per defective IC.

As the high roller at $40,822, MWH923 is analyzed further in the following matrix:

IC Std Part Number	Used per Assembly	Number of ICs Failed	Debug Costs
— 028	12	1,139	$14,820
— 047	1	58	744
— 027	2	143	1,852
— 029	1	115	1,488
— 012	5	456	5,928
— 015	9	797	10,374
— 011	4	259	3,370
— 471	1	86	1,123
— 472	1	86	1,123
Totals	36	3,139	$40,822

1,424 printed circuit boards were tested last month which gives the following failure rates and costs:

$$\text{Cost per failed IC} = \$40,822 / 3,139 = \$13.00$$
$$\text{Failure rate} = 3,139 \text{ failed ICs} / (1,424 \times 36) = .06122 = 6.1\%$$

An analysis of reasons for failure follows:

Infant Mortality	85%
Out of Tolerance	11%
All Else	4%

The commercial grade integrated circuits that we are using cost 50¢ each.

For an additional 50¢ each, Chi Square Test Lab proposes to screen out 90 percent of our potential failures.

Recommendation—More than $36,000 in gross savings will be realized by screening our integrated circuits (ICs) prior to stuffing them into our assemblies. Therefore we should try a pilot run by screening all of the —028 ICs, to determine if the actual savings realized will equal the 90 percent anticipated. A successful pilot run will signal full-scale screening.

Justification—$36,740 (90 percent of $40,822 debug costs) is the projected savings to result from screening all ICs.

The costs involved to realize these savings are $25,632 (1,424 Boards x 36 ICs/Board x 50¢ each).
- This leaves: $11,108 net savings projected
- Almost $5,000 will be saved in the pilot program

Gross Savings	= 14,820 x .9	= $13,338
Cost	= 17,088 ICs x 50¢	= $ 8,544
Net Savings		= $ 4,794

Based on the example above, the following message to management is appropriate. Note that the message is clearly stated in bottom line vernacular, pointing up the savings to be had.

This is the type of message that can be presented at the staff meeting on an overhead transparency. However, do not neglect to follow up with a formal justification and a plan of action to make the savings a reality.

The message to management:
— $11,000 in direct savings can be realized by screening our integrated circuits
— The pilot program to prove the savings plan has a potential

payback at $4,800. In other words, $8,500 in screening costs will eliminate $13,300 in debug or failure costs. (NOTE: $ amounts rounded.)

Summary of Principles
1. Cost of quality reports usually include the following:
   - Cover letter
   - Detailed cost summary
   - Trend charts

2. Use the high roller method to determine the areas where the most improvement can be effected.

3. Determine how improvements can be made.

4. Justify projected improvements by showing how savings versus cost add up to profit improvement.

5. Make management proposals in bottom line vernacular.

6. Systematize cost improvements by using action item groups, or some method of your own that is effective for your organization.

7. Top management sanction and support are the top priority.

CHAPTER 7

Organizing and Managing
for Improvement

The Improvement Program

Mounting an effective improvement program is often viewed as a somewhat complex and mysterious undertaking. Implementation of a large-scale improvement program could be a little complex, at least initially, but there need not be any mystery to the improvement process itself.

There are three essential ingredients needed to make any improvement program successful, regardless of the size and scope of the program: initially, you must have management commitment; without it even small successes will be difficult to achieve. Next, you must understand how to organize your resources to achieve the desired objective in the quickest and least expensive way possible. And finally, you must know how to implement and manage the improvement process.

Securing Management Commitment

As we have said many times in earlier sections, securing management commitment to the improvement program is essential to ultimate success. If you have followed our instructions in collecting, analyzing and reporting the quality cost data to management, you should be in a good position to secure their approval to go forward with improvement projects.

If you have done all that we suggested and are still unable to get management backing, we recommend you do the following: First and foremost, back off long enough to reevaluate the situation, i.e., let the dust settle and then take another look at where you are. Next, reach deep within yourself for answers to tough questions like the following:

- Did I do all the preparatory work that was needed?
- Did I present a logical, cost-effective improvement program plan?
- Did management understand what I was trying to tell them?
- Did management seem to have confidence in me?

If the answer to any of these questions is no, then go back to the beginning, revise your approach as necessary and try again. Perhaps, develop a new improvement program that is less ambitious, one they can commit to with less risk and that will let them build confidence in both you and the program.

If you have done all the additional things we have suggested and management still resists your pleas for support, then consider the possibility that you are out-of-step with company philosophy and current objectives. Evaluate this possibility very carefully because if you find that is the case, there are really only two choices—fall into line or seek a more cooperative environment elsewhere.

Organizing for Improvement

Organizing and mobilizing your resources for improvement will not be the least of your problems as you go about trying to reduce costs. It is important that you understand what forms of organization are available to you, as well as which ones are best suited to your specific purposes.

The following is an overview of the most common forms of organization used in implementing improvement activities, and a description of how and when each type should be used.

Task Force: As used here task force will mean a formal committee comprised of two or more people, usually from different departments within the company, who have been selected to pursue resolution of a given problem. The scope of the problem, however, will most certainly affect the number and type of people who are appointed to the task force.

When the problem is defined in a broad sense, such as overall reduction of quality costs, the task force will usually consist of major department heads (e.g., manufacturing, engineering, quality assurance and so on) who will serve as the steering committee. In addition, one of these department heads will be appointed as the task force leader (or chairman), and will be responsible for coordinating task force activities and reporting. It is also likely that additional members from each department will be appointed to subcommittees (or action item groups) and will be responsible for working on smaller portions of the problem. This type of task force is normally employed when a major improvement program is underway.

When there is no formal improvement program in force, a more limited form of task force is usually employed. In this event, the purpose of the committee is very narrow and is often limited to only a few action items. This type of task force is very similar to the action item group described below.

Action Item Group: An action item group normally consists of two or more individuals who are responsible for addressing only the top one or two of the quality cost factors at a time. Only the top contributor is worked on to assure that this one item gets all of the attention needed to reduce it until it is not a major contributor anymore. Action items need to be resolved by managers who will directly be affected by the solutions.

Generally, the action items should be those which promise the greatest improvement for the least amount of effort. However, low yield items can be included, especially if they are easy to handle. Successful conclusions to even the simplest problems are great for morale and tangible proof that all of the other jobs can be done.

Other Methods: Task forces can be used while one of the other methods is working or they can operate independently. However, you are free to choose the system or systems that work best in your situation.

For instance, you may wish to do something as different as assigning one person as a quality cost reducer and let this person do analysis, corrective action and everything. When done this way, the person should be able to get any help that he or she needs from any branch and any level of personnel. Incidentally, this last method has essentially described the system where top management gives whole-hearted endorsement to the improvement of quality costs.

Implementing the Improvement Process

Now that you have learned how to go about securing management approval and organizing your resources to accomplish your cost reduction objectives, it is time to learn more about the improvement process and its implementation.

The improvement process as defined here will include only those basic elements that form the common thread linking virtually all definitions currently supported by most quality professionals. We have chosen to relegate the subjects of management commitment and organization for improvement to the broader concept of the improvement program. This has been done to simplify our presentation of information, and to promote better understanding of each of the three major components involved in achieving general improvement. With this in mind we may now proceed with defining each of the major steps required in implementing and sustaining the improvement process.

Define Problem: Before attempting to make any kind of change it is important to understand the nature of the problem. The quality cost data that has been collected should give strong indications of where to look first. By using a Pareto analysis technique and doing some investigative legwork it should be a relatively simple matter to identify the problem and its root causes. A word of caution. Be certain to define the real problem, not just the symptom.

For instance, if your investigation indicates that the sloppy workmanship exhibited by the assembly department is the probable result of a department supervisor who lacks the proper attitude toward quality and pride of workmanship, then say so. Don't simply blame the assemblers for doing sloppy work.

Identify Solution: Once the problem and its causes have been identified, you must decide what should be done about it. Consider all your options and be sure to evaluate each using the cost justification techniques described in earlier sections. Here again, you must be careful to develop and propose solutions that address the real problem and its causes, not the symptoms.

Using the example of the assembly department, our concern can be easily illustrated. If you had concluded that the problem was simply the result of sloppy workmanship by assembly personnel, then you logically would assume that some form of quality training and/or workmanship certification program would correct the problem. What a waste of time and money that would be, since these people would be returning to exactly the same environment that caused them to produce sloppy workmanship in the first place. Instead you should recommend some form of corrective action that will either promote or induce the proper attitude change in the supervisor. *Don't avoid addressing the real issue!*

Secure Approval: In many cases no special approval beyond the scope of your own authority is required. This is often the case when there is no formal improvement program underway. If you have the authority and the ability to approve implementation of the corrective action, then do so without delay. If, on the other hand, the proposed solution has the potential to seriously impact company activities or there is a formal improvement program in force, you have an obligation to inform management of your recommendations and seek their approval prior to implementation.

Implement Solution: Put the authorized changes into effect.

Monitor (or audit) Effectiveness: All too often changes are made without anyone ever checking to see whether they have had the desired effect or if they were discarded after a period of time. It is extremely important that this step be performed periodically. Initially, the audit should be directed at assessing how effective the change has been in achieving the desired results. You will sometimes find that while the solution looked very good on paper or was quite logical based on the data, it simply didn't work. If this is the case, start the process over again.

On the other hand, even solutions that are effective initially may be rendered ineffective by other changes that occur over time, or they may simply be ignored by those who didn't like the change in the first place.

Major changes should be monitored at the end of each reporting period for the first three to six months, and quarterly after that. Minor changes should be monitored for at least the first several months.

Repeat the Process: The improvement process is a never-ending cycle. Even if none of the other variables changed, it would be reasonable to expect that many iterations of the process might be needed before results could be maximized. While in the general sense this is true, there is nonetheless a need to determine the logical point at which further improvement should be abandoned.

The logical point to stop seeking additional improvement is usually referred to as the point of diminishing returns, which means that the cost of obtaining the additional improvement is equal to or more than the anticipated benefit. In quality cost terms this point has been reached when the major quality cost categories have achieved the desired balance, and there are no improvement projects that will do better than break even.

Managing the Improvement Process

Tracking improvement activities can be a time-consuming task, especially in the case of large-scale improvement programs. However, it is also one of the most important activities contributing to the overall success of the program. You will find that it is very easy for the program, and those responsible for its implementation, to stray off course and fall behind schedule. The only way to safeguard against this is to closely monitor progress for each of the various activities.

For informal or small-scale improvement programs, tracking may consist of nothing more than a list of who is supposed to do what and by what target date. The larger, more complex improvement programs will probably require the use of more sophisticated tracking techniques such as Gantt or PERT (Project Evaluation and Reporting Technique) charting. If properly used, these techniques will serve as excellent tools in monitoring and controlling the progress of improvement activities.

One of the most difficult disciplines to maintain during the improvement process is that of properly documenting the improvement activities. There will be great pressure to close action items as quickly as possible, especially when management is actively participating in reviewing improvement activities. Everyone wants to look good in management's eyes. In addition to this pressure, it is also true that many simply do not like being closely scrutinized by management and will seek to end such scrutiny as quickly as possible.

We recommend the following documentation be generated any time a formal improvement program is undertaken:

• Develop an action item list that contains the following information:

Problem: Develop a clear and concise statement of the problem to be addressed. Be sure to revise this statement whenever necessary to accurately reflect the addition of new data. You may find that this will sometimes be necessary as a result of additional information (data) discovered while implementing the corrective action.

Action: Specifically define the corrective action to be taken. If necessary, develop a complete implementation plan. If the problem definition is revised for any reason, then reevaluate and revise the corrective action statement as necessary.

Responsibility: Identify, by name, the person who is responsible for the implementation of this corrective action. Even when several individuals may be directly involved in performing the necessary activities for implementation, it is important that one person be assigned as the responsible party for coordinating and reporting progress. Do not assign responsibility to an organization, because if you do, no one will be obliged to take direct responsibility.

Implementation Date: This is normally the date upon which the responsible person formally declares the implementation complete. This should be done in writing, and addressed to the task force leader or steering committee. Also, it would not be unusual to have two different date blocks instead of one. The first block would be the target implementation date, and the second would be the actual implementation date.

Follow-up Responsibility: Name of person who was assigned the responsibility for performing a follow-up audit of this corrective action.

Follow-up Date: This is the date upon which the assigned auditor declares the implementation to be satisfactorily completed and verified.

Closure Date: The date upon which the task force leader determines that all implementation requirements specified by the corrective action have been met (including all closure documentation requirements). This action item is officially closed.

• Develop and maintain, for future reference, a file containing the following closure documentation as objective evidence of corrective action activities:

— Summary documents containing problem definitions and corrective actions, including copies of modifications made to either of these.

— List of personnel involved in implementing the corrective action and associated task force activities.

— Formal statement of implementation, signed and dated, from the person assigned the responsibility for implementing the corrective action.

— Formal statement of verification, signed and dated, from the person assigned the responsibility for performing the follow-up audit.

— Copies of all procedures, drawings, engineering changes and sketches of any tools, fixtures, etc., that were changed or developed for the purpose of meeting the specific requirements of the corrective action.

The last key ingredient in successfully managing an improvement program is reporting of results to management on a timely and realistic basis. You will have to be careful here because there is a common tendency to overdo the reporting. If you do overreport on the program, you will quickly lose management attention. As a general rule, management does not have the time to pore over reams of detailed information and reports, and will quickly abandon any attempt at doing so. To avoid this problem we suggest the following guidelines:

• Report limited status on a monthly basis, i.e., action items closed and problems that may delay progress on other action items. Keep reports as simple as possible. Provide summaries of the activities whenever complex programs are being reported. Include the details only as a backup to the summaries, and then only if management has expressed an interest in seeing them.

• Provide a major program review quarterly. This is the proper time and place to point out the successes of the program, and to seek management assistance in removing or resolving open issues that will inhibit progress.

• Whenever target dates for completing specific tasks are to be included in reports or program reviews, be extremely careful not to underestimate how long it will take to complete the tasks. Explain delays or snags clearly and honestly. Don't make excuses, just state the facts.

• Do not overstate the successes of the program, because to do so will reduce your credibility.

• Give credit to those who deserve it, and be aware that this will reflect well on you.

Summary of Principles

1. For securing management sanction, always relate proposed improvements to the bottom line.

2. Initially, any improvement program will cause a rise in total quality cost. Monitor program for lower cost trends by way of measuring the effective improvement.

3. Attack major cost items (most fruitful areas) first. After major cost improvements, continue searching for more cost improvement projects.

4. Devise a measurement system to show improvement project effectiveness.

5. Give credit to individuals and teams for progress shown.

6. The improvement process consists of the following steps:
   - Define problem
   - Identify solution
   - Secure approval
   - Implement solution
   - Monitor effectiveness
   - Repeat the process

CHAPTER 8

Tuning the Quality Cost System
for Added Profit

The Optimum Cost of Quality

So far, everything presented has been aimed at helping you to get a significant reduction of your costs of quality. Perhaps your cost ratios will even be somewhat balanced, compared to the ratios at the beginning of your program. Now it is time to begin the optimization process. Now you will find profit improvement to be more difficult to achieve, but it is still possible to squeeze many more dollars out of your quality costs. As you do so, you will move closer to achieving your optimum.

The usual question at this point is how do we know when our optimum total quality cost has been achieved? The answer, unfortunately, is not straightforward. Since, as we have already pointed out, there are no industry standards to guide you in your efforts to achieve the optimum, you will have to rely heavily upon the empirical evidence of your past data and the experience you have gained during the operation of your cost of quality program. The only additional guideline that we can offer is that, as a general rule, your quality costs may be considered optimal when the cost categories are balanced and there is an absence of profitable projects that will further reduce your overall costs.

The rest of this chapter talks about the steps you should take when you encounter the various ratios between cost categories as you go through the optimization phase.

Balanced Cost Categories

In general, a company has an acceptable quality cost relationship when the total failure costs are about equal to the prevention and appraisal costs. This may not be true for companies such as those which are making components to be used in space—it is obvious that the next-to-perfect performance required of items which can't be repaired must depend on appraisal. There are also instances where less than perfect quality may be the ruin of the company. Food processors may dump an entire factory's six-month output rather than risk even a few cases of food poisoning. Pharmaceutical companies and medical device makers likewise strive for perfection.

Aerospace companies brag, "We do 100 percent inspection and test!" But what they really mean is that they look at each part at least eight times! The parts are first tested at incoming inspection. They are tested again before they are used in the subassembly. Then again as part of the subassembly. The subassembly is tested before it is put into the assembly—then again as part of the assembly—and at least two more times before they go into the final assembly, where they are tested at least one more time as a part of the whole. Perfect product, not optimum quality cost balance, is the natural aim for the aerospace industry as well as the food, drug and medical device people.

However, for most companies, failure costs[†] equal to appraisal and prevention costs is the usual signal that they have reached the plateau in their quest for optimizing their profits by control of the expenses that will go away when they are able to make everything right the first time, and every time. When the quality cost system is more or less in balance, there is a tendency to let down. But this is not the signal to sit back and enjoy a job well done. The potential savings may not be as spectacular as was found earlier in the program, but there is still much room for improvement. Some ideas for more profit improvement follow:

1. Look around for ways to continue your cost reduction crusade. As an example, certification of vendors could be a highly profitable project. The cost of installing a statistical process control system in a vendor's plant would provide a handsome return on investment in reduced receiving inspection costs and reduction of inventory costs.

2. Plan for less expensive ways to maintain your control of the costs of quality. Examples of further cost reductions of this kind follow:

• Use statistical process control instead of inspection. This will enable corrective action to be taken before the process begins to make parts outside the specification limits.

• Use frugal sample plans or auditing instead of MIL-STD-105 inspection for verification of quality. As the product quality increases, much smaller samples can be used to assure the maintenance of quality.

• Use continuous quality verification instead of lot sampling. Or install a skip lot sample scheme.

With a little ingenuity, the actual control can be maintained, or even increased while the inspection task is being reduced. In looking at the cost of quality graphs (Figs. 16 & 17) these observations can be

[†]For detailed discussion see *The Quality Control Handbook,* Third Edition, Juran

made: the general trend for the cost of quality, as a percent of revenue, appears to be beneficial; quality costs were high at the first of the year, although in general, they were balanced; in 12 months the overall cost of quality has been reduced to one-fourth; evidently, this company is making progress in tightening their control of quality costs. Good job—well done—keep up the good work!

NOTE: The total cost of quality graph is indexed only as a percent of revenue. The rule of thumb is for two bases for comparison, but this has been ignored for this demonstration to make the trend easier to visualize.

r = % of Revenue

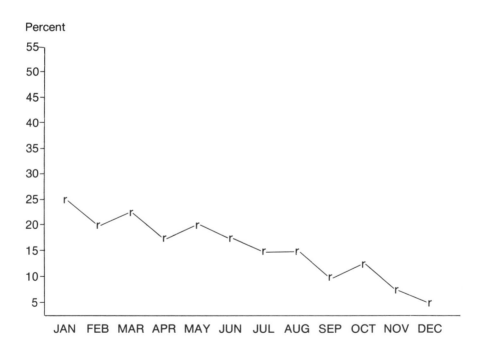

Figure 16 — Total Cost of Quality (COQ) Trend Chart

Failure Costs Too High (Refer to Figs. 18 & 19)

When failure costs are more than 60 percent of the total for all categories, it is usually the signal to spend more money on prevention and appraisal. Obviously indiscriminate spending in these categories

p = Prevention Costs
a = Appraisal Costs
i = Internal Failure Costs
x = External Failure Costs

Percent

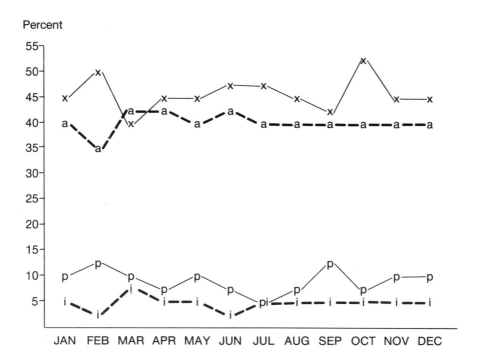

Figure 17 — Major Cost of Quality (COQ) Trend Chart

will balance the system, but the total cost of quality will also increase. This is not the solution.

Before doing anything, the payback should be investigated. A negative payback could be acceptable for the reduction of failures, but this should not be the rule. Happily, since good quality is less expensive, investigation and planning before spending almost always result in an overall profit improvement. As a matter of fact, the rare circumstances of no change in the imbalance without an increase in the total may be an early indication that this particular imbalance is the optimum for your company.

A general plan for bringing the ratio of the failure costs into line with the costs of prevention and appraisal follows:

• Use Pareto or other analysis to choose a project for

improvement. An especially fruitful starting place is the return area of your plant.

• Plan your attack on whatever failure cost factor you have chosen. Analyze how much it will cost to make your plan work. Estimate how much will be saved.

• Justify your plan. In other words, do a return on investment study to show the ratio of payback to expenditure. Be sure to include your estimate of the overall savings.

• Sell your plan in bottom line language. If possible, tell management how much the profits will increase when breakthrough is a reality.

• Implement the plan and pursue the project with vigor, until breakthrough is achieved.

In looking at the quality cost graphs, Figures 18 and 19, the following observations can be made:

1. Trends are hard to determine from looking at these graphs—we might try graphing the figures as a three-month rolling average to see if the trends will show up better.

2. It appears that the costs of quality are almost in balance by the end of the year, but this is mainly due to the increasing trend of the appraisal costs.

3. It is difficult to determine if the program is effective, since the overall trend for the total cost of quality (as a percentage of revenue)

---

r = % of Revenue

Percent

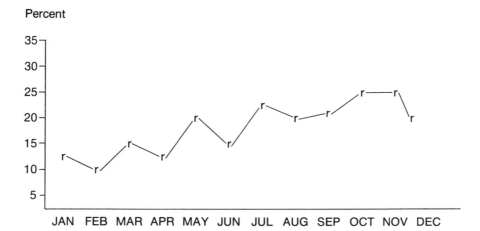

Figure 18 — Total Cost of Quality (COQ) Trend Chart

is rising. Graphing the cost figures as a percent of manufacturing costs or costs of sales might enhance our view.

4. It is time to investigate our projects to see if we are close to breakthrough or if our estimates of savings were in error. Another area of investigation is the actual process of the collection of data. It may turn out that we are actually getting better results on our cost of quality, but are looking worse because we are getting better at finding those costs which were previously camouflaged or buried in the accounting system.

5. Although our results are mixed, it is not time to quit. One area where savings might be found is to make appraisal efforts more efficient.

Appraisal Costs Too High (Refer to Figs. 20 & 21)

When appraisal costs are more than 50 percent of the total of the

---

p = Prevention Costs
a = Appraisal Costs
i = Internal Failure Costs
x = External Failure Costs

Percent

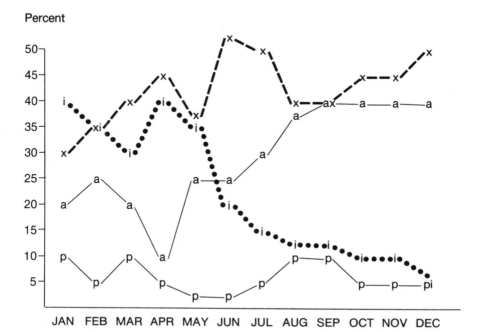

Figure 19 — Major Cost of Quality (COQ) Trend Chart

quality costs, it usually means there is no understanding (or trust) of statistical quality control and statistical process analysis. Too much inspection is being performed; sample sizes are too large; screening of lots is being done too often, and the like.

One example of too much test (appraisal) is the violation of the one percent rule by semiconductor users. It costs about as much to test 100 parts before assembly as it does to find one bad part at test after assembly. Yet many companies struggle for perfection by screening 100 percent instead of sampling to assure an outgoing yield of good parts at 99.3 percent, (the added .3 percent is not really needed, but can be viewed as insurance against the spread of probabilities involved in the sampling).

Analysis of the cost of finding defects will often show that the trade-off indicates the standards should be relaxed or the same or better results can be had by much less inspection. Alternate methods of control should be investigated.

Statistical quality control methods can be looked on as a periodic

---

m = % of Manufacturing Costs

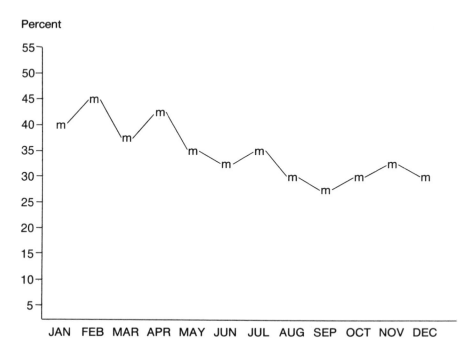

Figure 20 — Total Cost of Quality (COQ) Trend Chart

audit designed to assure the manufacturing process is in control and to furnish warning signals when corrective action is needed. Statistical process control methods are even better, since this method signals corrective action *before* the process is out of control. Look for ways to relax standards for noncritical parameters while continuing to prevent the major and critical defects.

In the case of failure costs being too high, the inability to find the key for balancing the ratio for quality costs may be a sign indicating that optimum for your company is slightly off center. Remember there are no reliable industry standards. Therefore, your own historical and trend data are the best guides for measurement.

In looking at Figures 20 and 21, these trends are observed:

1. Generally, the ratio of internal to external failure cost appears about where it should be.

---

p = Prevention Costs
a = Appraisal Costs
i = Internal Failure Costs
x = External Failure Costs

Percent

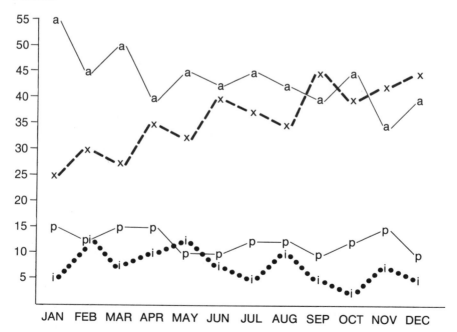

Figure 21 — Major Cost of Quality (COQ) Trend Chart

2. Likewise the ratio of prevention cost versus appraisal cost seems about right.

3. The overall quality cost figure (as a percentage of manufacturing cost) has declined about 25 percent during this 12-month period.

4. During this same period, the ratio between failure costs and prevention and appraisal costs has begun to come into line.

5. All of the foregoing leads us to believe that in general, appraisal costs have been reduced with little or no increase in the failure costs.

Summary of Principles

1. Total failure costs should be about equal to the cost of prevention plus the cost of appraisal.

2. The ratio between external failure and internal failure costs should be about 9 to 1.

It must be stressed at this point that a 9 to 1 ratio of external to internal failure costs does *not* mean a 9 to 1 ratio of external to internal failure *occurrences*. On the contrary, the number of external failure occurrences must be no more than a small fraction— preferably zero, of course—of the number of internal failure occurrences. However, because it is so much more—perhaps a hundred times more—expensive to correct a defect in the field than to correct the same defect in the plant, even a few defects that "escape" can result in considerable expense.

3. The ratio of appraisal to prevention costs should be about 4 to 1.

4. The ratios of principles 1, 2 and 3 are guidelines only and may be somewhat different for your organization.

It should also be noted at this point that there is little agreement in industry regarding ratios between quality cost categories. The ratios used here have been utilized in real companies, but other ratios may be more appropriate for your company. In analyzing quality cost ratios and trends you are the expert—pay attention to other experts only when they agree with what *you* think is best for your company.

CHAPTER 9

Postscript: Reducing White Collar Overhead

Introduction

One much overlooked opportunity for profit improvement involves controlling quality costs associated with white collar activities. Most literature on the control of quality costs is devoted entirely to manufacturing applications. However, basic principles of quality cost control are as applicable to white collar environments as they are to manufacturing.

Greater emphasis will be placed on controlling white collar quality costs during the coming years as the service sector of our economy continues to expand and, according to many economists, overtakes manufacturing as our most important business activity. With this change in direction will come increased concern about administrative and clerical activities, and improved techniques for measurement and control of these areas.

For a manufacturing company in today's operating environment, the white collar costs (both quality and nonquality in nature) are what constitute the overhead burden rate we discussed earlier. As you may remember, overhead is usually several times larger than the direct costs associated with producing and delivering a product. With this in mind it is easy to understand how even relatively small improvements in overhead burden rates can significantly contribute to profits.

In the balance of this section we will discuss how quality cost techniques and principles can be applied to white collar activities.

White Collar Quality Costs

White collar quality cost issues are not very different from those found in normal manufacturing situations. For instance, an assembly worker may occasionally miswire a component while building an electronic assembly, or a clerk may inadvertently insert an important document in the wrong envelope. Both errors will result in inconveniencing the customer if not discovered prior to delivery of the product or service, and both errors will also require extra effort to correct the situation. In the case of the assembly error, someone will have to debug the assembly to determine the problem, and additional time will be spent in correcting the miswire. As for the clerical error, someone will have to determine what happened to the original document, and additional time will be spent in preparing another document for mailing to the correct client.

If you doubt the existence of white collar quality costs, just look around your office for a while and ask yourself why it was necessary for your company to spend thousands of dollars in providing word processing equipment for clerks and secretaries. Surely, someone who types at a rate of 55 wpm on a typewriter will type no faster on a word processor. However, it is much easier and quicker to correct mistakes on a word processor than a conventional typewriter, and that reduces the quality costs associated with typed materials. Ask yourself why it is necessary for formal documents to be typed and retyped an average of three times before they're finally acceptable, or why the file you've been looking for isn't where it's supposed to be.

These, of course, are just a few examples of white collar quality costs, and we do not mean to single out clerks and secretaries as the main contributors to white collar quality costs. Managers, engineers and administrative personnel make mistakes that result in lost time and money.

How to Measure White Collar Quality Costs

There are a number of techniques that can be used to measure and collect the costs of quality in white collar environments including random-time sampling, self-analysis and statistical process control. The following brief overview of measurement techniques is based on Harrington's *Poor Quality Cost* (see Bibliography), which is recommended reading for those who desire more information.

Random-Time Sampling: This technique requires use of a trained observer who audits the activities of people within a department or work area.

Self-Analysis: Self-analysis can be performed in either of two ways. The first method is by using personal logs on which employees record their activities in each of the five designated categories (i.e., basic work, prevention, appraisal, internal failure and external failure activities). The second method involves use of department activity logs which require that employees define the department's mission, major activities and intended customer for each activity. When done properly this method can be most effective since it results in developing detailed specifications for input as well as output, and sets minimum performance standards.

Statistical Process Control: This method of measuring performance within white collar activities would be implemented in much the same way as in a manufacturing area. Control charts with appropriate limits would be used to indicate whether the components within a given business process are stable and within acceptable performance limits.

How to Report White Collar Quality Costs

Reporting of quality costs must begin, by necessity, with the development of a chart of quality cost accounts. There are relatively few rules to restrict your development of such a chart to suit your company's needs. However, the rules that do exist, such as those summarized below, should be carefully observed in order to promote comparability between similar companies reporting quality costs.

- Maintain four basic categories of quality costs:
— Prevention
— Appraisal
— Internal Failure
— External Failure

- Use as many subcategories as necessary to adequately isolate major cost factors, but do not go overboard. It isn't necessary to have a subcategory for each possible cost factor; try to logically combine them whenever it makes sense to do so.

- Thoroughly define each category and subcategory so that everyone understands what is meant by the title.

A sample chart of quality cost accounts for a company specializing in providing word processing services is shown in Figure 22. Please note that the sample chart of accounts is consistent with the above stated rules.

Once a satisfactory chart has been established, any of the previously mentioned measurement techniques may be used to collect, or estimate, the costs in each subcategory. Analysis of the data should be handled in the same way that manufacturing cost data was handled in Chapter 5. It doesn't matter that this data comes from a white collar environment, the analytical techniques are the same. All that remains then is to report these costs to management with appropriate recommendations for improvement.

The report format to be used should be no different from that described in Chapter 6. The same basic elements must be applied to reporting of white collar quality costs as were applied to manufacturing quality costs. The basic principles of reporting are once again presented below:

Cover Letter: Quality cost trends should be noted and

TYPICAL CHART OF QUALITY COST ACCOUNTS

PREVENTION

101 Quality System Planning — Develop and maintain quality system documentation detailing process flow checkpoints and instruction.

102 Review Customer Order — Review customer's order for clear description of work to be performed, and completeness of specific instructions.

103 Prepare Job Specification — Prepare detailed specification describing desired format (i.e., headings, spacing, footnoting, page numbering, etc.) for use by operator and checker.

104 Data Analysis — Monitor process and customer complaint data for ongoing compliance to accepted quality performance standards. Also includes all time expended to record process performance and preparation of charts.

APPRAISAL

201 Proofing — Initial inspection of drafted materials for completeness, proper format, typos and misspellings, and general compliance with customer's specified requirements, etc.

202 Quality System Audit — All time and related expenses associated with verifying the adequacy and compliance of the quality system.

203 Maintenance — All expenses incurred in maintaining the quality of equipment used in word processing and duplicating activities, i.e., replacement of worn print heads and similar items, etc. Does not include the cost of routine expendables such as ribbon and duplication chemicals, etc.

INTERNAL FAILURE

301 Reprocessing — All word processing resulting from the need to correct inaccuracies and misspellings, etc., found in the initial draft. Does not include revisions made at the customer's expense.

302 Reproofing — Inspection of revised material resulting from errors found in the initial draft.

303 Downtime — All time lost as a result of inoperative equipment or incomplete work instructions.

EXTERNAL FAILURE

401 Reprocessing — All word processing resulting from the need to correct errors found by the customer.

402 Reproofing — Inspection of redrafted material resulting and analyzing customer complaints.

403 Customer Complaint Adjustment — All time spent reviewing and analyzing customer complaints.

404 Customer Allowances — The cost of price reductions intended to induce customers to accept substandard work.

Figure 22 — Chart of Accounts

improvement areas should be identified. A good distribution plan would be a monthly report with a review of the improvement program's progress included in the end-of-the-quarter letter.

Detailed Cost Summary: Costs are best presented in tabular form with comments concerning short-term and long-term trends. Improvement suggestions should be included even when the trend line seems to be beneficial (i.e., how to make the trend even better).

Trend Charts: These charts are the graphical presentation of the quality cost data. Trends are easy to spot on graphs and a chart showing beneficial trends is a great motivator for continuation and more effort toward the improvement project program.

Control and Improvement of White Collar Quality Costs

You have come, once again, to the main point of our discussion. After all, the main objective of a cost of quality program is not the collection and analysis of data. The main objective is the reduction of costs so profits can be increased.

Implementing and managing an improvement program to reduce white collar quality costs can be accomplished by applying the principles outlined in Chapter 7. The basics are summarized as follows:

• Appoint an individual or a committee (i.e., a task force, or action item group) to take responsibility for reviewing, analyzing and recommending corrective action.

• Regularly report the progress of appointee(s) in conducting the necessary research and ensure that all activities are documented.

• Submit proposals for corrective action to management for approval prior to implementation.

• Periodically review (or audit) the effectiveness of corrective actions that have been implemented.

• Repeat the process until there appear to be no profitable projects remaining and cost of quality categories are balanced.

Summary of Principles

1. White collar quality costs are usually included as burden or overhead and added to their appropriate quality cost element.

2. White collar quality costs are a gold mine for improved profits, but in most cases should be attacked after major cost items have been reduced.

3. Extreme care and planning must be used in any program to improve white collar efficiency because of the politics involved.

AFTERWORD

Plan the Work,
Work the Plan

The principles of cost saving and increased quality/reliability as described in this book are universal. They are as applicable to your home life and your avocations as they are on the job. Using these principles, you can develop a plan for determining and handling a cost of quality program for your college, your church, the local hospital or a community organization. Even an organization designed as a not-for-profit operation can make gains in the quality of its services and achieve cost savings by following such a plan.

Your ability to visualize new and different uses for Pareto analyses is one of your greatest tools for reducing the costs of quality. It is a valuable asset that can directly lead to increasing productivity and profits and improving the quality of your life and work.

It is important to remember that good quality is not more expensive but is universally cheaper than poor quality, and that holds true for services as much as for manufactured products.

Plan the work of analyzing costs carefully and in full detail (what, when, who, why, how). Your plan should conform to the other operating procedures of your company or organization as closely as possible in order to assure cooperation and success.

Develop a feel for what is, or is not, a legitimate quality cost. Consistently sort costs for careful analysis and learn to make valid judgments about their avoidability.

Once you have identified the quality costs, make certain you use all the graphic sales tools to chart and illustrate your findings. These graphic tools are invaluable in delineating problem areas and in demonstrating potential profit improvements in order to gain and maintain continued management support for your plan. Management will soon recognize the power of quality cost tabulation to improve profits and will begin initiating their own analyses.

Continue to work the plan even when success is apparent. Prepare detailed trend charts and summaries in periodic reports with a cover letter that points up the more notable quality cost trends, long and short term, and foreseeable problem areas. Remember, management normally spends little time with lengthy, overdetailed explanations. Make the report concise and graphic, but include improvement suggestions even when the trend line is favorable. In other words, suggest how to make the trend even better.

If you are not getting the management support you deem necessary for success of the program, do some deep soul-searching and objectively analyze your plan. Did you do the necessary preparatory work? Does management fully understand your plan? Is your program possibly out-of-step with company philosophy and current long-range and short-term objectives? Can your plan be revised to fall in step and gain support?

Remember *you* are the expert and who can redesign the plan better than you? Regard information or opinions from others as something that *you* must verify and evaluate for yourself. A plan based on faulty assumptions will not have a strong enough foundation to resist the many natural detractors that will pop up along the way.

You are the expert and you are armed with the tools that can build a system that can help you make a difference in the quality of your company's future and affect your life and everyone that your quality plan touches.

APPENDIX A

QUALITY COST WORKSHEETS
Appraisal Costs Worksheet

I. Incoming Material Inspection
   1. Receiving inspection . . . . _____
   2. Source inspection. . . . . _____
   3. Surveillance . . . . _____

II. Inspection and Test
   1. In process . . . . _____
   2. Final accept . . . . _____
   3. Packaging . . . . _____
   4. Shipping. . . . . _____
   5. Life test . . . . _____
   6. Environmental test . . . . _____
   7. Reliability test . . . . _____
   8. Field test . . . . _____

III. Maintaining Accuracy of Test Equipment
   1. Operation . . . . _____
   2. Calibration . . . . _____

IV. Materials
   1. Destructive test . . . . _____
   2. Consumable materials . . . . _____

V. Services
   1. Facilities, power, water, etc.. . . . . _____

VI. Evaluation of Stocks
   1. Stores inventory . . . . _____
   2. Shelf life . . . . _____

TOTAL APPRAISAL COSTS: _____

Prevention Costs Worksheet

I. Quality Planning

1. Quality plan . . . . _____
2. Inspection plan. . . . . _____
3. Reliability plan. . . . . _____
4. Data system . . . . _____
5. Other specialized plans . . . . _____
6. Quality manual . . . . _____
7. Procedures. . . . . _____

II. New Products Review

1. Preparation of bid proposals. . . . . _____
2. Evaluation of new designs . . . . _____
3. Preparation of test and experimental programs . . _____
4. Other new product quality activities . . . . . . _____

III. Training

1. Preparation of training programs . . . . _____
2. Conducting the training program . . . . _____

IV. Quality Data Acquisition and Analysis

1. Data collection. . . . . _____
2. Data analysis . . . . _____
3. Quality reporting. . . . . _____

V. Other Prevention Activities

1. Process control. . . . . _____
2. Improvement projects. . . . . _____

TOTAL PREVENTION COSTS: _____

Failure Costs Worksheet

I. Internal Failures

1. Scrap . . . . _____

2. Rework . . . . _____

3. Retest . . . . _____

4. Downtime . . . . _____

5. Yield losses . . . . _____

6. MRB activities . . . . _____

II. External Failures

1. Complaint adjustment . . . . _____

2. Returned material . . . . _____

3. Warranty charges . . . . _____

4. Allowances . . . . _____

TOTAL FAILURE COSTS: _____

APPENDIX B

SAMPLE COST OF QUALITY PROCEDURE

1.0 SCOPE:
This procedure describes the general requirements for collection and evaluation of quality cost data, and is applicable to all operating divisions, products and services of this corporation.

2.0 PURPOSE:
To establish a system for identifying and controlling costs related to quality.

3.0 REFERENCE:
3.1 Attachment I—Quality Cost Account Codes

4.0 DEFINITIONS:
4.1 In general, quality costs are defined as follows:
All expenses which are incurred in the assurance and control of the manufacture of products which meet the customer's requirements. In other words, the cost of quality could be visualized as those expenses which would not exist if we were able to design and build products which were totally free of defects.
4.2 The four major quality cost categories are defined as follows:

4.2.1 *Cost of prevention*—Costs incurred for maintenance of a quality program that will ensure overall requirements are met at a minimum cost.

4.2.2 *Cost of appraisal*—Costs incurred in measuring and assessing products, materials and components to ensure they meet acceptable levels.

4.2.3 *Cost of internal failures*—Costs associated with products, materials and components that fail prior to shipment.

4.2.4 *Cost of external failures*—Costs that are incurred after acceptance and failure of finished products at customer's on-site location.

5.0 GENERAL:
5.1 The accounting department shall be responsible for collecting and compiling cost of quality data for distribution to management.
5.2 The quality assurance department shall be responsible for reviewing and analyzing cost of quality data, and for providing a written overview of indicated trends as well as recommendations for corrective actions of noted problems.
5.3 Reported costs shall be based on general ledger and labor

distribution accounting records where possible.

5.4   Where accounting records do not provide sufficient detail, estimates may be used to assign relative costs to each category.

    5.4.1   In no event shall the sum of individual subcategories exceed the costs supported by accounting records for the major category. Example: If the total expense for quality assurance activities during the reported period was $1,000, then the total could be divided into several subcategories such as data acquisition and analysis, quality planning and Material Review Board (MRB) activities, but the total, no matter what the distribution of costs, could not exceed $1,000.

5.5   In those cases where accounting records do not collect the information, such as rework costs and most MRB costs (except scrap), then independent data collection apparatus shall be established by quality assurance.

5.6   For ease of collection and reporting the quality cost data, the subcategories may be combined or separated in any fashion that permits both accuracy and clarity.

5.7   Overhead allocation for labor and material expenses shall be applied using a burden rate of 2.5.

5.8   The cost of quality report shall be prepared and distributed on a monthly basis.

6.0   PROCEDURE:

6.1   Accounting shall compile and submit the cost of quality data to quality assurance within 10 working days after month end.

6.2   Quality assurance shall review and prepare a written analysis of the data within five working days after receipt from accounting.

6.3   The data shall be reported using the preformatted forms below:

    6.3.1   Quality Cost Summary

    6.3.2   Total Cost of Quality Trend Chart

    6.3.3   Major Cost of Quality Category Trend Chart

6.4   The final draft of the monthly cost of quality report shall be submitted to the manager of quality assurance for final review and approval prior to distribution to management.

6.5   The cost of quality report shall be distributed as follows:

    6.5.1   Chief Executive

    6.5.2   Finance Manager

    6.5.3   Engineering Manager

    6.5.4   Operations Manager

    6.5.5   Marketing and Sales Manager

ATTACHMENT I

TYPICAL QUALITY COST ACCOUNT CODES

The following are detailed descriptions and account codes for each of the cost subcategories that comprise the four major quality cost categories:

PREVENTION CODES

110   Quality Planning—The time personnel devote to system planning, inspection planning and test engineering. This subcategory also includes the costs incurred by other departments whose personnel participate in quality planning activities.
120   Process Control—The time personnel devote to process implementation, capability studies and special process studies.
130   Quality Training—Process technology training, technical training, quality control techniques training and certification programs.
140   Vendor and Material Control—Vendor surveys, corrective action and source surveillance.

APPRAISAL CODES

210   Product Test—Including subassembly test, assembly test, final test and customer acceptance.
220   Inspection—Includes time spent by personnel in evaluating product conformance in manufacturing, and time spent by personnel verifying the quality of purchased materials or services.
230   Equipment Calibration and Maintenance—Time spent by lab personnel in the calibration and maintenance of equipment, records and related costs.
240   Quality Audits—System and product audits, and related planning and evaluation activities.

INTERNAL FAILURE CODES

310   Scrap—Costs associated with materials that are scrapped due to nonconformance to requirements.
320   Rework—Labor and material costs expended to bring nonconforming products to acceptable levels of quality.
330   Reinspection—Labor and material costs expended to verify conformance of reworked products.
340   Retest—Labor and material costs expended to test reworked products.

EXTERNAL FAILURE CODES

410   Complaint Adjustment—All costs of investigations and adjustment of justified complaints attributable to defective product or installation.
420   Returned Material—All costs associated with receipt and replacement of defective product returned from the field.
430   Warranty Charges—All costs involved in service to customers under warranty contracts.
440   Allowances—Cost of concessions made to customers due to substandard products being accepted by the customer. Includes loss of income due to downgrading of products for sale as seconds.

APPENDIX C

QUALITY COST ACCOUNT STRUCTURE

General Labor Account Codes

SECTION A: PREVENTION

Includes charges and salaries of all personnel when performing the following activities, internally or at vendor's facilities:

101 **Analysis and Planning for Quality and Reliability**

Defining product-related requirements, such as reliability, maintainability and safety, service life, acceptance specifications, reliability specifications, inspection planning, etc. Defining requirements and implementing programs generally related to quality and reliability, such as certification plans, reliability plans, vendor control plans, material handling plans, audit plans, quality policies and procedures, etc. Reviewing quality, reliability and safety aspects of product designs.

104 **Process Control Analysis**

Analysis of manufacturing equipment and processes to improve capability and performance and to establish controls. Providing technical support for and to shop personnel in applying quality, reliability and safety programs in resolving potential quality problems and in developing control over manufacturing processes.

107 **Process Control Certification**

Determining and/or certifying the quality capability of processes or equipment.

110 **Process Control Audits**

Auditing the effectiveness of the quality, reliability and safety system controls. Conducting all aspects of preaward surveys, of purchase order review and of vendor rating for quality and reliability. Analyzing all data for quality, reliability and safety definition or improvement purposes.

113 **Specification, Design and Development of Quality Information Equipment**

Specifying and developing product and process measurements and data requirements, and designing and developing product and process measurement and control devices and related equipment.

116 **Quality Training and Manpower Development**

Developing, conducting and evaluating planned programs intended to orient and train all personnel as appropriate in the comprehension and use of programs and techniques for the control of quality, reliability and safety. Providing formal quality performance certification of operators, inspectors and testers, as required. (Includes salaries and wages of personnel attending formal training sessions.) Providing for improvement in promotion and management potential of all quality-related personnel.

119 **Product Design Verification—Inspection and Test**
Inspection and testing of product for the purpose of verifying the quality, reliability and safety aspects of the design.

122 **Product Design Verification—Material and Equipment**
Associated material and equipment.

125 **External Quality Systems Development**
External engineering and management support for systems development.

128 **Other Prevention Costs**
Quality and reliability organizational costs not otherwise accounted for, such as managerial and clerical salaries, travel expenses, rent, etc.

SECTION B: APPRAISAL
Includes charges and salaries of all personnel when performing the following activities, internally or at vendor's facilities:

201 **Test and Inspection of Purchased Material**
Inspection and test evaluation and reporting the quality of purchased materials. (Does not include retest, reinspection or sorting because of defectives.) Related supervisory and clerical costs. (QA Department only). Costs of resident or transient source inspection or vendor surveillance.

204 **Laboratory Testing—Purchased Materials**
All costs of laboratory testing and analyses of purchased materials for initial acceptance of all selected receipts. (Does not include retesting of rejected or reworked material.)

207 **Laboratory Testing—In Process and Finished**
All internal and external laboratory costs associated with the evaluation of products in process or finished. (Does not include retesting of rejected or reworked material.)

210 **Laboratory/Measurement Costs—Quality Equipment**
All maintenance component and gage laboratory costs associated with monitoring, calibration, maintenance and repair of all quality information equipment, standards and production equipment that generate quality characteristics. Laboratory

costs associated with preparation, preservation and transportation of pertinent equipment to storage or external facility (e.g., National Bureau of Standards). (Includes the cost of evaluating tools, gages, etc., in storage.)

213   **Field Equipment Calibration and Maintenance**
All costs associated with the calibration and maintenance of field equipment.

216   **Quality Control Inspection**
All costs associated with the inspection of tools, equipment and processes by quality control personnel (including product during processing, finished product and packaging and packing materials and methods.)

219   **QC Clerical and Supervisory Costs**
Associated costs of quality control clerical and supervisory activities.

222   **Production Inspection and Test**
Costs incurred by production personnel in the evaluation and reporting of the quality of in-process or finished product for which they or other operating personnel are responsible (does not include reinspection or sorting because of defects.)

225   **Quality Assurance Process Test of Products and Packaging**
All costs associated with the testing of processes, products during processing, finished product and packaging and packing materials and methods. (Does not include retest or sorting because of defectives.)

228   **QA Clerical and Supervisory Costs**
Associated costs of quality assurance clerical and supervisory activities.

231   **QA Occupancy Costs**
Occupancy costs for the quality assurance department.

234   **Materials and Supplies for Inspection and Test**
Includes all costs of materials and supplies consumed in performing inspection and test activities.

237   **Purchase and Installation Costs—Quality Information Equipment**
Purchase and installation costs of quality information equipment such as procurement, construction, rental, depreciation and EDP charges.

240   **Quality Audits—Process and Production**
In-process control, special processing, inspection of product, test of product, inspection and test of received product, inspection and test of packaging and packing and customer-centered audits.

243 **Quality Audits—Vendors**
All costs associated with auditing vendor processes, products, etc., including salaries, travel costs and living expenses.

246 **Outside Endorsement Costs**
Includes all costs and fees associated with external agency approval, e.g., Underwriters Laboratories, insurance inspection and tests, government agencies.

249 **Field Inspection and Test—Product**
Field inspection and test of product at the customer's site prior to final release—in negotiations to support such testing; also includes wages, salaries, travel costs, living expenses and equipment rentals for field testing.

252 **Inspection and Test—Field Stocks**
Inspection and test of field stocks such as product, components or parts for deterioration or damage.

SECTION C: INTERNAL FAILURE
All costs (including shop overhead) of items scrapped or reworked, and labor expended because of engineering, manufacturing, quality, vendor or similar error, specifically the following:

301 **Scrap—Engineering Change**
Scrap resulting from implementation of an engineering change order (ECO.)

304 **Scrap—PCB Repair Parts**
Defective parts removed from a printed circuit board assembly.

307 **Scrap—Chance Failures**
Scrap caused by a chance failure of an assembly or component part.

310 **Scrap—Mishandling**
Scrap caused by mishandling of an assembly or component part.

313 **Scrap—Operator Error**
Scrap resulting from an operator error.

316 **Scrap—Process Error**
Scrap resulting from a process error.

319 **Scrap—Purchase Defectives/Company Error**
Scrap caused by the incorrect purchase of unreturnable material resulting from company error.

322 **Scrap—Lost Parts**
Lost parts (inventory shrinkage adjustment).

325 **Scrap—Other**
Other (i.e., destructive test). Does not include obsolete stores, new requirements or overruns not made for quality reasons nor

any costs listed under Additional Operations—Defective Product.

328 **Rework—Engineering Change Order**
Rework resulting from the implementation of an engineering change (ECO).

331 **Rework—Chance Failures**
Rework caused by the occurrence of a chance failure.

334 **Rework—Mishandling**
Rework caused by the mishandling of assemblies or component parts.

337 **Rework—Operator Error**
Rework caused by an operator error.

340 **Rework—Process Error**
Rework resulting from a process error.

343 **Rework—Purchase Defectives/Company Error**
Rework caused by the incorrect purchase of unreturnable material as a result of company error.

346 **Rework—Other**
Other (i.e., equipment incompatibility). Does not include reprocessing or obsolescent stores, nor any costs listed under Additional Operations—Defective Product.

349 **Material Value—Defective Vendor Product**
Replacement value of defective vendor material.

352 **Wages and Salary—Defective Vendor Product**
Wages and salaries of personnel involved in reprocessing or repairing defective vendor products.

355 **Disposition and Corrective Action—Defective Vendor Product**
Procurement costs in obtaining disposition and proper corrective action including notification costs.

358 **Handling and Transportation—Defective Vendor Product**
Handling and transportation expenses, handling damage assessment.

361 **Vendor Failure Analysis Charges**
Failure analysis charges by vendor.

364 **Sort/Retest—Defective Vendor Product**
Sort, retest, etc. Not including any costs listed under Additional Costs—Defective Product.

367 **Investigate Defect Cause—Defective Product**
Defect cause examination: Data generation and analysis. Resolution of quality, reliability and safety problems and revision of the following: product designs, process, patterns, molds, tools, jigs, fixtures, gages; equipment (including machine tapes) and system controls.

370 **Additional Operations—Defective Product**
Reinspection, retest, and sorting, additional manufacturing, inspection and test operations.

373 **Product Disposition—Defective Product**
Costs associated with disposition of product, including Material Review Board (MRB) actions.

376 **Evaluation of Corrective Action—Defective Product**
Evaluation of effectiveness of corrective action. (All because of defective product, including scrap and rework.)

379 **Downtime—Quality Problem**
Time lost due to quality problems.

382 **Downtime—Insufficient Preventive Maintenance**
Costs of equipment downtime resulting from inadequate preventive maintenance.

385 **Downtime—Lack of Machine Capability**
Cost associated with machinery and equipment being unable to produce parts within tolerance.

SECTION D: EXTERNAL FAILURE

All costs associated with addressing and rectifying customer complaints, specifically the following:

401 **End User—Investigation/Repair/Service**
Costs of investigation, analysis, repair and service.

404 **End User—Allowances**
Allowances including customer abuse or misapplication.

407 **End User—Machine Replacement**
Machine replacement costs including freight.

410 **End User—Investigation/Noncompany Problem**
Investigation of noncompany problems.

413 **End User—Engineering Change Installation**
Cost of field installation of engineering changes.

416 **End User—Field Modification Bill**
Cost of field modification bills, including material and handling charges.

419 **OEM—Investigation/Negotiate/Analyze**
Costs associated with investigation, negotiation and analysis of customer complaints.

422 **OEM—Repair/Technical Assistance/Service**
Costs of providing technical assistance, repair and service.

425 **OEM—Allowances**
Allowances, including customer abuse or misapplication.

428 **OEM—Machine Replacement**
Machine replacement costs, including freight charges.

431   **OEM—Field Modification Bill**
Cost of field modification bills, including material and handling costs.

434   **OEM—Other Vendor Problems**
Other vendor problem at customer site.

437   **Product Liability Costs**
Includes the following costs: insurance costs, legal actions, reliability and safety claims and consequential damage costs.

443   **Field Failure Reporting**
Includes factory support for summarizing and reporting technical data, but excludes routine field technical support personnel.

446   **Spares Carrying Cost**

449   **Spares Usage**

QUALITY COST ACCOUNT STRUCTURE
ENGINEERING LABOR ACCOUNT CODES

SECTION A: PREVENTION

101   **Product Planning**
Initiating, defining, specifying, reviewing and negotiating of quality, reliability and/or safety requirements for new or revised equipment, materials, processes and/or products. Such activities as defining and estimating quality, reliability and safety requirements, service life, data and control error rates, acceptance criteria are included when they relate to the planning aspects of product designs.

104   **Manufacturing Process Technical Support**
Any technical support provided to manufacturing for improving company or vendor's processes that have been developed and relate to the quality, reliability and/or safety of company products.

110   **Audit of Quality System Controls**
Any audit of the effectiveness of either company or vendor quality, reliability and/or safety system controls; conducting all aspects of preaward surveys and of vendor rating for quality and reliability (e.g., component engineering work in vendor surveys and approving components and vendors for the Approved Vendor List—AVL).

113   **Quality and Reliability Test Equipment**
Specification, design and development of manufacturing test equipment including test software for the measurement or

monitoring of quality, reliability and/or safety of products.

119 **Preproduction Product Test (Design Review)**
Any independent preproduction inspecting and testing for verifying quality, reliability and safety aspects of the design. These activities are separate and distinct from the original design and are normally not done by the original designer. Such activities as worst case analysis, tolerance studies and environmental tests are included, but only when done as a post-design review.

SECTION B: APPRAISAL
246 **Regulatory Agency Evaluations**
Any preparation or assistance on tests to obtain approval from outside agencies such as Underwriter's Laboratories, CSA (Canada), GPO (UK), VDE/FTZ (Germany), Japan, etc. This does not include either initial design or redesign time to conform to the standards.

249 **Field Test**
Field inspection and test of product at the customer's site prior to final release, or in negotiations to support such testing.

SECTION C: INTERNAL FAILURE
367 **Defect Cause Investigation and Resolution**
Investigation and resolution of any problems relating to quality, reliability and safety of company products in production. This will primarily be Request For Analysis (RFA) and Engineering Changes (EC). Those actions intended for cost savings purposes do not apply.

373 **Disposition of Product**
Any time spent on MRB activities by development engineering.

419 **OEM Field Technical Assistance**
Any technical assistance to the field that relates to quality, reliability and/or safety problems and are not either repair (422) or other vendor (434) problems (e.g., compatibility problems).

422 **OEM Field Technical Assistance—Repair**
Any technical assistance that relates to the repair of an OEM product.

434 **OEM Field Technical Assistance—Other Vendor**
Any technical assistance to the field that turns out to be caused by non-company equipment.

SECTION D: EXTERNAL FAILURE

401   Field Technical Assistance
Any field technical assistance that relates to end-user quality, reliability and/or safety problems of company products.

410   Field Technical Assistance—Noncompany
Any technical assistance that relates to end-user quality, reliability and/or safety problems that turn out not to be caused by the company's products.

QUALITY COST ACCOUNT STRUCTURE
FIELD SERVICE ACCOUNT CODES

SECTION A: PREVENTION

101   Includes salaries and charges of all personnel when performing the following activities: initiating, defining, specifying, reviewing and/or negotiating of quality, reliability, safety or serviceability requirements for new or revised equipment, materials, processes and/or products. Such activities as defining or reviewing and estimating quality, reliability and safety requirements, service life, data and control error rates are included when they relate to the planning aspects of product design for maintainability and forecasting.

SECTION B: APPRAISAL

213   Activities associated with field equipment calibration and maintenance.

252   Inspection and test of field stocks of products, components or parts for deterioration or damage.

SECTION C: INTERNAL FAILURE

367   All wages, salaries of personnel involved in supporting defect cause investigation that occurs at any manufacturing facility. This would include data generation and analysis for the resolution of quality, reliability and safety problems and revision of the following: product design, process, patterns, molds, tools, gages, equipment (including machine tapes) and systems controls.

SECTION D: EXTERNAL FAILURE

401   Investigation, analysis, repair, service on specific field complaints for end-user equipment.

410   Investigation of noncompany problem on specific field complaint for end-user equipment.

413   Labor cost associated with installation of an engineering change on end-user equipment.
419   Investigation, negotiation, analysis on specific field complaints of OEM customers.
422   Repair, technical assistance, service on specific field complaints of OEM customers.
434   Wages, salaries of personnel involved with investigation of non-company problems at OEM customer site.

Bibliography and Recommended Reading

Poor Quality Cost, H.J. Harrington, Marcel Dekker, Inc., 1987.

The Quality Control Handbook, Third Edition, J.M. Juran, McGraw-Hill, 1971.

Quality Is Free, Philip B. Crosby, McGraw-Hill, 1979.

The Statistical Control of Quality, Parts I and II, Dr. W. Edwards Deming, Quality magazine, February and March, 1980. (Available as a reprint from: Quality, Hitchcock Publishing Company, Wheaton, Illinois 60188.)

Total Quality Control, Third Edition, Armand V. Feigenbaum, McGraw-Hill, 1983.

Work Sampling, R.E. Heiland/W.J. Richardson, McGraw-Hill.

AT&T Statistical Quality Control Handbook, Western Electric Co. (AT&T), 1956.

Quality Management Handbook, Walsh et. al., Marcel Dekker, Inc., 1986.

Customer Satisfaction through Total Quality Assurance, Grenier, Robert, Hitchcock Publ., 1988.

BOOK TWO

The Quality Cost Workbook

Section I   **Life Cycle Costs**
Section II   **Cost of Quality Exercises**
Section III   **Pareto Analyses and Matrices**
Section IV   **Cost of Quality Analyses**
Appendix   **Answers and Comments**

HOW TO USE THE WORKBOOK

The work exercises contained in this workbook are designed to help you put to use the principles described in Book One. Make up a worksheet titled at the top with the name of the assignment, e.g., "I. Work Assignment 1: Sharing of Excess Life Costs" and write your answers on these worksheets as an aid in working out actual problems. If you are conducting the workbook exercises with a group, make an overhead transparency slide with the appropriate headings and write in the group's answers as they are discussed.

When you have completed the work exercises in Book Two, compare your answers with the authors' answers and comments. Each workbook section has a matching Appendix, beginning with Appendix I (matching Section I) on page 122.

The authors' assignments are based on actual experiences. While some of the questions do have technically correct answers, others are open-ended and the reader's analysis, based on sketchy details, may be just as valid as the authors' analysis or recommendations. In real life, the quality manager will face problems that will differ in the details, but the purpose of the exercises is to understand the principles involved. When a principle is in doubt, review the appropriate section in Book One.

SECTION I

Life Cycle Costs

I. Work Assignment 1
Sharing of Excess Life Cycle Costs

Federal Trucking Company is about to equip half their gasoline-powered trucks with the Electron-John electronic ignition system. Electron-John has stated that there will be a savings of 10 percent of routine maintenance and fuel.

Federal has 213 gasoline-powered trucks and has been considering a program to phase out their gasoline engines in favor of diesel power, since their diesel fleet averages 8 percent less for routine maintenance and fuel than their gasoline-powered units. Last year, routine maintenance (i.e., repairs, lube, oil and fuel but not tires, brakes or accidents) totaled $8.5 million for the 213 gasoline-powered trucks.

Electron-John has proposed converting 100 trucks at a cost of $400,000. This cost includes a one-year maintenance policy.

Federal has decided to include the following paragraph in their proposed contract with Electron-John:

> The Electron-John Company will guarantee, as a contractual item, a savings of 10 percent. This savings will be determined by direct comparison of routine gasoline and maintenance costs for our units with and without Electron-John ignition installed. In the event that actual savings are less than 8 percent, Electron-John agrees to absorb half of any unrealized savings in maintenance and fuel costs below 8 percent. This stipulation will be in effect for the first year only and the maximum rebate will be limited to half the value of the contract.

Please give your analysis of this situation for Federal.

Questions:

a. Is Federal making the correct decision?

b. What is the appropriate action for Electron-John?

c. What would you recommend for either or both of these companies, from your outside viewpoint?

I. Work Assignment 2
Rebate Based on Excessive Failures

Federal Trucking Company is considering the installation of a combination telephone/truck-log module in each of their trucks during the next 12 months. The module consists of a conventional mobile telephone, with the added capability for sensing and storing running time, speed and other truck-log information. It will be equipped with a digital-data processor for daily transmission of truck-log information to the home office. The unit design includes slow-scan television circuitry, but this is not intended for immediate use.

Federal has not made a firm decision because they are not sure of the reliability of the module. Therefore, they have drafted what they believe to be a fair reliability assurance clause:

> *The telephone module is made up of a central processing unit (CPU), a video section (VID), a slow-scan television (SST) circuit with printer, the truck-log unit (TLU) and a power supply (P/S). Federal technicians will maintain all installed modules and will require training and spare parts advice from the supplier.*

> *Should there be 2 percent or more failures of the CPU, the VID, the TLU or the P/S in any one month (200 hours of operation) or 5 percent or more failures of any of these units in 2,400 hours of operation (one year), the supplier will redesign the module as required to reduce the incidence of failures.*

> *Any design changes will be incorporated on all new units. Kits or exchange units will be supplied to retrofit all installed modules. These requirements will be part of the module's warranty for the first two years after delivery.*

Please give your analysis of this situation.

Questions:

a. Will the proposed Federal clause do the job they want it to do?

b. How would you respond if you were working for a supplier bidding on the job?

c. From your outside viewpoint, what would you recommend as a course of action to either Federal or to a prospective supplier?

I. Work Assignment 3
Cost-Sharing Based on Degenerative
Mean Time Between Failures (MTBF) Trends

Original Unit Research Inc. (known as OUR Company) manufactures peripheral equipment for personal computers. OUR Company is negotiating with a personal computer manufacturer who wants to market OUR Company's new "THREE-DEE-JOY-STICK" under his label (he plans to call it "3-D Stick," his own trademark). Their initial offer is for 20,000 units per month for the first year with option to double the delivery rate at any time during the year. At the lower rate, this job will amount to $250,000 per month gross sales for OUR Company, which by itself is about half of OUR Company's present gross.

OUR Company's only problem is that the computer company wants a cash guarantee clause relating to Mean Time Between Failures (MTBF). Specifically, they want OUR Company to return 1 percent of the total value of the contract for every 100 hours that the demonstrated MTBF falls below 15,000 hours. They will limit OUR Company's liability to 50 percent of the contract. Of course, they would terminate the contract if it ever reached that point.

On the surface, this offer seems fair, since OUR Company's calculated value of the MTBF for the THREE-DEE-JOY-STICK is 31,820 hours. Also, OUR Company will have access to the computer company's field data, and the way they calculate the demonstrated MTBF is acceptable.

Please give your analysis of this situation.

Questions:

a. With what action or decision should OUR Company respond to the computer company's request for an MTBF guarantee?

b. Should OUR Company believe the computer company's field data, which they plan to use to demonstrate the MTBF?

c. What is the probability that an MTBF guarantee would put OUR Company into Chapter 11?

I. Work Assignment 4
Design Review Based on Life Cycle Estimates
Problem 4a: Institution

The Customs area at Gotham City International Airport has been deemed inadequate for a long time. The Gotham City Chamber of Commerce has often voiced its opinion that Europeans coming to the United States usually choose another port of entry because Customs at Gotham City has the reputation of being little less than harassment. In spite of Gotham City's stringent customs reputation, a Chamber of Commerce official has stated "The F.B.I. still points out that this airport is a major entry point for illegal goods arriving at the U.S. East Coast by air."

Gotham City plans to add a new international wing to the airport. U.S. Customs will install a new facility which will include all of the latest technology. The criteria listed below for the new facility are based on costs of similar installations, updated for inflation and adjusted for location. You are under contract to the General Services Administration (GSA) to conduct periodic design reviews as an extra effort to make Gotham City the most efficient U.S. port of entry. The estimated life of the facility is 12 years.

(All cost estimates are in millions of dollars)

Cost of 10-gate facility. $27.0
Maintenance cost, per gate, per year . . . . $ 0.8
Manning cost, per gate, per year . . . . $ 1.45
Please give your thoughts concerning the proposed facility.

Questions:
a. What topics should be addressed in the conceptual design review? The conceptual design review is defined as the first design review, when the design is still in block diagrams or sketch form and the final cost figures have yet to be approved.

b. Use Life Cycle Cost as a tool to help your analysis.
   — Determine the cost for each gate for the 12-year life of the facility. (Multiply maintenance and manning costs for each gate by 12.)
   — Add these costs to the cost of the 10-gate facility for the total life cycle cost.
   — Use these figures to help establish your agenda.

Problem 4b: Support Van

Several fuel pump systems which have been proposed for the standby electrical system in the support van for a Super-Speed Mini-Recon plane are listed below:

1. Pump is driven by an electrical motor which can operate on 110 volts AC or 6-, 12- or 24 volts DC. (Cost estimate: $25,000. A motor-driven pump driven by AC or DC alone is estimated to cost $20,000.)

2. Pump is driven by the standby electrical system's gasoline motor, fueled by the system's last gallon of fuel. (Cost estimate: $10,000. For safety reasons, the fuel tank for the standby electrical system has been limited to five gallons of gasoline. The costs of the design change required to add an extra gallon volume to the tank would be about $2,000.)

3. Both pumps (from items 1 and 2) in redundancy, to cover all events of happenstance and failure.

Please analyze the various proposals. Add any ideas of your own.

Questions:

    a. How would you outline your agenda for the design review?

    b. Would you propose any other solutions to the problem?

Summary of Principles

1. Life cycle costs add up the total costs for using the item.
2. Total life costs are valid for comparison and trade-offs.
3. There are many new applications for life cycle costing.
4. Life cycle costing is seldom used for quality improvement but more and more it is a technique being used to force future design changes.

SECTION II

Cost of Quality Exercises

II. Work Assignment 1
First Estimate of Quality Costs

You are the new quality director for Leptran Manufacturing Company. As near as you can tell, Leptran has had no quality cost program in the past.

You have been looking around the factory, especially in the material review crib where the field returns are impounded. From your observations, you estimate that the returned material amounts to at least 10 percent of the total of the goods sold each month.

When you confront the vice-president of manufacturing, he disclaims this 10 percent figure. "We used to have more than 10 percent returns," he says, "but now it's down to less than 2 percent!"

Leptran's profit and loss statement for last year indicates a 4 percent profit based on sales of $21.1 million.

You check the return area again, and believe that your original figures are correct. Either the vice-president of manufacturing doesn't know what is going on or he is deliberately camouflaging the data.

Questions:

a. Can you make any estimate of Leptran's true quality costs?

b. Do you think you have enough evidence to start a quality cost program?

c. Can you make any projections as to Leptran's profit improvement that you can bring about?

d. Outline the steps that you would take to initiate such a program for Leptran.

II. Work Assignment 2
Elementary Cost of Quality Analysis

Last month, after rummaging through Leptran's accounting records for a single month and making a few independent guesstimates, you developed the following quality cost figures:

Inspection and test wages	$ 29,000
Burn-in and final test	56,000

Quality planning	6,300
Audit	2,000
Calibration (outside lab)	4,000
In-plant scrap	4,000
Rework	3,000
Complaint adjustment	25,000
Warranty reserve	21,000
Material Review Board costs	700
Field returns	104,000

You estimate that 40 percent of the burn-in and final test cost is due to repairing and retesting units that failed during burn-in. Also, 20 percent of inspection and test time is for reinspection of reworked or repaired items.

You know that your burden factor is 2.2 (i.e., the actual wages are multiplied by 2.2) to account for a fair share of the administrative costs and white collar wages.

Questions:
a. Based on these figures, what is your best estimate for the following quality cost categories?

Prevention costs	_____
Appraisal costs	_____
Failure costs	_____

b. What is your estimate of the ratio of internal to external failure costs in this company?

c. If this company shipped $2.2 million worth of products last month, what is your assessment of the health of this company?

II. Work Assignment 3
Estimating, Synthesizing and Tabulating Data for the Analysis of Cost of Quality Trend Charts

Leptran Manufacturing Company did not have a quality cost program before you came to work for them. Six months ago, based on your analysis of returned product, you were given the go-ahead to start some kind of a program. You have been gathering data for the past six months, and plan to make your first definitive analysis of Leptran's quality cost early in July, to coincide with the start of Leptran's fiscal year. It is now mid-June and you have collected the following data:

January: So far, Leptran's field returns for January total $156,000. You think this is 90 percent of the total that will accrue against warranty for January. Revenue for the month is $1,757,000. Manufacturing costs were $387,000. Cost of sales was $875,000.

February: Field returns for February total $111,000. Past records indicate that this will be about 70 percent of the warranty total. Revenue for February is $1,767,000. Manufacturing costs were $371,000. Cost of sales was $884,000.

March: March field returns to date are $68,000. This is guesstimated to be about 40 percent of the total that will come in against March shipments. Revenue for March was $2,195,000. Manufacturing costs were $465,000. Cost of sales were $1,104,000.

April: Revenue for the month was $1,920,000. Administrative salaries for the month totaled $6,300 without burden. The burden rate is 2.2. You have decided to allocate this expense as follows:

Quality planning	40%
Test engineering	30%
Reliability engineering	20%
Data crunching	10%

Quality and test wages were tabulated as follows:

Inspection (24% for reinspection)	9,000
Test (40% for debug and rework)	20,000
Audit	2,000

The burden rate for all these is 2.2. Other April costs were tabulated as follows:

Cost of manufacturing	$382,000
Cost of sales	834,000
Scrap	3,500
Rework	3,500
Complaint adjustments	14,000
Calibration services	4,000
Warranty reserve	21,000
Material Review Board costs	700
Field returns (estimated at 35% of total)	37,000

May: Revenue for May was $1,889,000. Other costs were tabulated as follows:

Cost of manufacturing	$361,000
Cost of sales	873,000
Administrative salaries	5,400
Inspection wages	8,800
Test wages	16,000
Audit wages	2,000
Scrap costs	3,200
Rework costs	2,200
Complaint adjustments	18,000

Calibration services	4,000
Warranty reserve	21,000
Material Review Board costs	900
Field returns (estimated at 25% of the total)	20,000

June: Revenue for June was $2,300,000 (projected). Other costs were as follows:

Cost of manufacturing (est.)	$450,000
Cost of sales (est.)	1,100,000
Administrative salaries	5,200
Inspection wages	8,800
Test wages	16,000
Audit wages	2,000
Scrap costs (est.)	2,500
Rework costs (est.)	2,500
Complaint adjustments (est.)	18,000
Calibration services	4,000
Warranty reserve	21,000
Material Review Board costs (est.)	1,000
Field returns (est.)	97,000

Based on these data, complete the following work assignments:

a. Make a cost of quality analysis spread sheet for the second quarter (April, May, June).

b. Synthesize the data and make a cost of quality analysis spread sheet for the first quarter (January, February, March).

c. Make a total cost of quality trend chart for January through June.

d. Make a major cost of quality trend chart by category for these months.

e. Prepare a presentation for Leptran's Chief Executive Officer and his staff concerning the financial health of Leptran Manufacturing Company based on the quality cost trends.

f. Prepare a cost of quality program plan (Procedure) for Leptran Manufacturing Company.

3a. and 3b. — Cost of Quality (COQ) Analysis Format
(see page 38 for sample)

Date _____   Quarter _____   Revenues _____

	Actual Expense	Burden Rate	Total Expense	Cost of Quality Category as Percent of			
				Total Cost of Quality	Revenue	Cost of Sales	Cost of Mfg.
PREVENTION COSTS							
Q E Planning							
Test Engineering							
Reliability Eng.							
Data Acquis. & Analysis							
Total Prevention Costs			_____	_____	_____	_____	_____
APPRAISAL COSTS							
Inspection							
Production Test							
Calibration Service							
Quality Audit							
Total Appraisal Costs			_____	_____	_____	_____	_____
FAILURE COSTS							
Internal Failure Costs							
Assembly Rework							
ECO Rework							
Inspection Rework							
Test Debug & Rework							
Material Review Board							
Total Internal Failure Costs			_____	_____	_____	_____	_____
External Failure Costs							
Complaint Adjustment							
Returned Material							
Warranty Charges							
Allowances							
Total External Failure Costs			_____	_____	_____	_____	_____
TOTAL FAILURE COSTS:			_____	_____	_____	_____	_____
TOTAL COST OF QUALITY:			_____	_____	_____	_____	_____

II. 3c.   Total Cost of Quality (COQ) Trend Chart

NOTE: The blank worksheets in Book Two may be photocopied for your convenience in completing the assignments. Additional copies are available from Hitchcock Publishing Company, Wheaton, IL 60188; phone 312/665-1000.

r = % of Revenue
s = % of Sales
m = % of Mfg Costs

Percent

100
90
80
70
60
50
40
30
20
10

JAN   FEB   MAR   APR   MAY   JUN   JUL   AUG   SEP   OCT   NOV   DEC

Analysis

	JAN	FEB	MAR	APR	MAY	JUN	JUL	AUG	SEP	OCT	NOV	DEC
Revenue												
Cost of Sales												
Cost of Mfg												
Cost of Quality												
Cost of Quality as percent of:												
Revenue												
Cost of Sales												
Mfg												

NOTE: Multiply all dollar figures by 1,000

II. 3d.   Major Cost of Quality (COQ) Trend Chart

p = Prevention Costs
a = Appraisal Costs
i = Internal Failure Costs
e = External Failure Costs

NOTE: The blank worksheets in Book Two may be photocopied for your convenience in completing the assignments. Additional copies are available from Hitchcock Publishing Company, Wheaton, IL 60188; phone 312/665-1000.

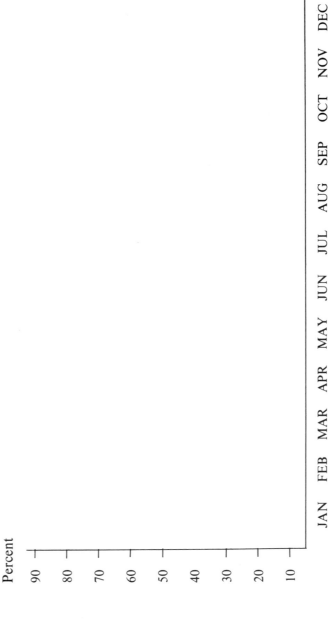

Percent

90

80

70

60

50

40

30

20

10

JAN   FEB   MAR   APR   MAY   JUN   JUL   AUG   SEP   OCT   NOV   DEC

Analysis

	JAN	FEB	MAR	APR	MAY	JUN	JUL	AUG	SEP	OCT	NOV	DEC
Percentages												
Prevention												
Appraisal												
Internal Failure												
External Failure												

Summary of Principles

1. In the beginning, there is usually very little quality cost data available. Usually, one must use estimates and secondary data.

2. A good first estimate of total cost of quality is made by doubling the value of the goods returned.

3. One of the best standards to measure against to determine cost of quality progress is past history.

4. Past history is best revealed by:

- Indexing cost of quality against some base, such as revenue or manufacturing cost.

- Graphing the total quality costs as a percentage of the index.

- Graphing the individual categories of the cost of quality as a percentage of the total quality cost.

- Analysis of the graphs for: total quality cost trends; cost of quality categories ratios.

SECTION III

Pareto Analyses and Matrices

III. Work Assignment 1
Simple Pareto Analysis

For the month of December, Leptran Manufacturing Company's internal failure cost totaled $87,000. The largest element under this category was assembly rework and test at $42,000. Use the factors of this element which are listed below to make a Pareto graph. Use a graph format similar to the example below. See Chapter 5 for examples.

Factors:		
	Mother Board	$23,900
	Power Supply	12,100
	Memory Board	3,800
	All others	2,200
	TOTAL (Assembly Rework)	$42,000

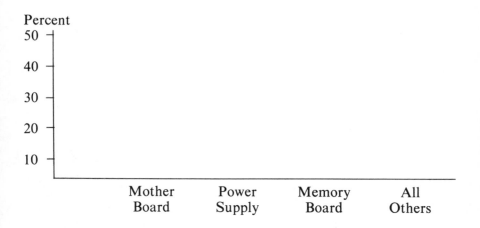

III. Work Assignment 2
Another Kind of Pareto Graph

For the month of December, Leptran Manufacturing Company's internal failure cost totaled $87,000. The second largest element under this category was test debug and rework at $33,000. Use the factors of this element which are listed to make a cumulative Pareto graph using the format shown below.

Factors:		
	Power Supply	$16,000
	Input-Output Board	9,800
	Mother Board	4,700
	All others	2,500
TOTAL (Test debug and rework)		$33,000

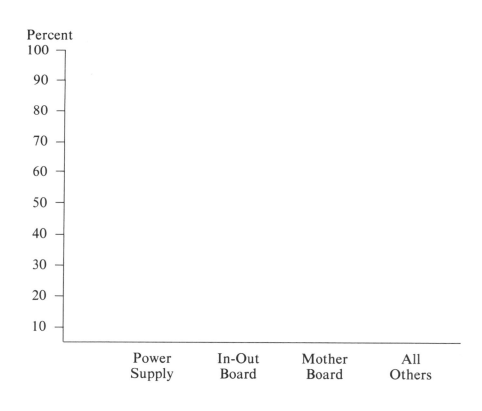

III. Work Assignment 3
Simple Matrix and Pareto Analysis

This multiple-part assignment will use both Pareto analyses and matrices. For samples of these problems, review Chapter 5. The defect data for this multiple-part problem follows:

Defect Descriptions (and code numbers)

Defect Code	Description	Defect Code	Description
1.	Wiring error	9.	Miscellaneous
2.	Short (actual or potential)	10.	Strapping error
3.	Wrong polarity	11.	Semiconductor
4.	Missing component	12.	Resistor
5.	Damaged component	13.	Capacitor
6.	Wrong value component	14.	Inductor
7.	Improper soldering	15.	Transformer-filter-relay
8.	Mistuned	16.	Lamp-switch

Codes 1 through 8 identify workmanship errors and codes 10 through 16 identify component-related subassemblies.

Defect Data

The test and repair group have listed all errors corrected or parts which were replaced.

Mother Board: 8 shorts; 14 missing components; 5 damaged components; 2 wrong value components; 10 strapping errors.

Power Supply: 1 improper soldering; 1 mistuned; 5 resistors; 7 filters.

Memory Board: 6 wiring errors; 2 wrong polarity; 9 wrong value components; 2 miscellaneous.

All others: 1 wiring error; 2 shorts; 1 wrong polarity; 1 missing component; 1 damaged component; 1 wrong value component; 1 improper soldering; 1 miscellaneous.

III. Work Assignment 3a-1
Simple Matrix

Use the graph below as a sample format to display the information above as a matrix. See page 29 for examples.

Assembly	1	2	3	4	5	6	7	8	9	10	11	12	13	14	15	16
Mother Board																
Power Supply																
Memory Board																
All others																
Totals																

III. Work Assignment 3a-2
Cumulative Pareto Analysis

Make a Pareto analysis to show defects by assembly from the information in 3a-1. Use the chart format shown in Work Assignment III. 2.

III. Work Assignment 3a-3
Cumulative Pareto Analysis

Make a Pareto analysis to show kinds of defects without regard to assembly, from the information displayed in the matrix in 3a-1. Use the chart format shown in Work Assignment III. 2.

III. Work Assignment 3b-1
Simple Matrix
Use the costs to repair for each defect below to make a new matrix similar to 3a-1.

Defect Codes and Costs to Repair

Defect Code	Description	Cost	Defect Code	Description	Cost
1.	Wiring error	$9	9.	Miscellaneous	$11
2.	Short (actual or potential)	2	10.	Strapping error	4
3.	Wrong polarity	3	11.	Semiconductor	10
4.	Missing component	5	12.	Resistor	1
5.	Damaged component	6	13.	Capacitor	1
6.	Wrong value component	4	14.	Inductor	1
7.	Improper soldering	1	15.	Transformer-Filter-Relay	7
8.	Mistuned	5	16.	Lamp Switch	2

III. Work Assignment 3b-2
Cumulative Pareto Analysis
Make a Pareto analysis to show cost of defects by assembly from the information of the matrix in 3b-1. Use the chart format shown in Work Assignment III. 2.

III. Work Assignment 3b-3
Cumulative Pareto Analysis
Make a Pareto analysis to show total cost of defects without regard to assembly, from the information of the matrix in 3b-1. Use the chart format shown in Work Assignment III. 2.

III. Work Assignment 3c-1
Simple Matrix

Use the criticality multiplier for each defect (shown below) to make a new matrix using the format shown in 3a-1.

Defect Codes and Criticality Multipliers

Code	Description	Criticality Multiplier	Code	Description	Criticality Multiplier
1.	Wiring error	3	9.	Miscellaneous	13
2.	Short (actual or potential)	2	10.	Strapping error	1
3.	Wrong polarity	2	11.	Semiconductor	15
4.	Missing component	4	12.	Resistor	1
5.	Damaged component	2	13.	Capacitor	2
6.	Wrong value component	2	14.	Inductor	2
7.	Improper soldering	2	15.	Transformer-Filter-Relay	5
8.	Mistuned	5	16.	Lamp-Switch	2

III. Work Assignment 3c-2
Cumulative Pareto Analysis

Make a Pareto analysis to show criticality of defects by assembly from the information of the matrix in 3c-1. Use the chart format shown in Work Assignment III. 2.

III. Work Assignment 3c-3
Cumulative Pareto Analysis

Make a Pareto analysis to show total criticality of defects without regard to assembly, from the information of the matrix in 3c-1. Use the chart format shown in Work Assignment III. 2.

III. Work Assignment 4
Freelance Pareto Analysis

Situation: The following is an "exception" printout of items scrapped during the month. The exception printout lists only those items that are more than $500 until the highest 10 items are listed. When there are fewer than 10 items over $500, the highest items less than $500 will be listed until there are 10 items.

Description	Number of Parts	Reason for Scrap	Amount
1. Cover Bracket	1,705	Engineering Change	$11,935
2. Top Cover (Lid)	415	Bad Finish, Blemish	12,429
3. Side Covers	346	Bad Finish	3,977
4. Front & Back Covers	391	Bad Finish	4,497
5. Frame	154	Bad Welds, Rust	5,708
6. Base Plate	333	Engineering Change	13,965
7. Harness, Misc. Wiring	686	Damaged Wires	1,583
8. Read-Write Heads	138	Cannot Align	3,181
9. Hard Disks	41	Magnetic Media Glitch	2,144
10. Floppy Disks	. 399	Excessive Soft Errors	339
Totals	4,608		$59,758

a. Identify the "high rollers." (Hint: Pareto-ize by failure cause.)

b. Plan corrective action for "high rollers."

c. Justify corrective action plan.

d. Prepare any message for management that you think to be appropriate.

Summary of Principles

1. The Pareto analysis makes it easy to choose the area which will probably yield the most return for effort expended.

2. Displaying data (especially failure costs) in a matrix makes it easy to "Pareto-ize" in two or more directions, e.g., by defect and by product.

3. Continued use of matrices makes it easy to Pareto-ize mentally in several directions, which helps to optimize the choice of the most fruitful areas for making quality pay.

SECTION IV

Cost of Quality Analyses

IV. Work Assignment 1
Analysis of Interruption of Manufacturing

The following are typical quality costs (partially-based on an actual case) where a manufacturing operation temporarily ceases. In this example, the plant was shut down and moved during the month of April. The revenue figures for April are carryover from previous months. The revenue shown for May, June and July reflect start-up in the new facility.

Other causes for interruption may be shutdowns due to automating, strikes, equipment replacement or other temporary stops in operation.

Make your analysis of the quality costs and other data listed here. Give your evaluation of the program and make any recommendations that you think warranted.

1. Note that the total cost of quality, before and after the "break" was never much lower than 10 percent of revenue.

Month	Revenue	Cost of Sales	Mfg. Costs	Prevention Costs	Appraisal Costs	Internal Failure Costs	External Failure Costs
Jan	8,458	3,383	1,692	116	604	279	283
Feb	10,583	4,233	2,117	122	416	283	279
Mar	15,088	6,035	3,018	151	743	292	297
Apr	2,083	3,451	1,717	227	578	156	349
May	5,015	2,006	1,241	121	606	207	308
Jun	7,820	2,013	1,564	153	742	324	417
Jul	7,565	3,026	3,026	114	609	376	218
Aug	10,583	2,117	4,233	121	590	336	261
Sep	14,923	5,969	2,985	148	742	386	358
Oct	12,742	5,097	2,548	120	601	275	324
Nov	12,776	5,110	2,555	121	426	338	279
Dec	16,965	6,820	3,393	153	750	292	452

All figures are in thousands of dollars.

2. Also note that the ratios of the cost of quality categories are out of balance.

IV. Work Assignment 2
Analysis of a New Company's Cost of Quality

Situation: You have been the director of quality for the Start-Up Company for about a month. During that time, you have estimated, audited and guessed your way to the set of quality figures below. You believe these figures to be at least 85 percent accurate.

Analyze these figures and base your Quality Plan for the next year on that analysis.

All figures are in thousands of dollars.

Data: Start-Up Company

Month	Mfg. Costs	Prevention Costs	Appraisal Costs	Internal Failure Costs	External Failure Costs	Total Cost of Quality
Jan	1,400	100	120	240	—	460
Feb	1,650	90	190	210	50	550
Mar	2,450	60	240	250	60	610
Apr	1,380	40	120	120	80	360
May	2,120	30	120	100	100	350
Jun	2,700	20	100	90	150	360
Jul	2,540	10	90	70	180	350
Aug	2,720	10	80	50	170	310
Sep	3,280	20	110	90	140	360
Oct	2,480	30	100	80	130	340
Nov	2,620	20	80	70	110	280
Dec	3,060	10	70	80	80	240

Use the charts on the following pages to graph the total cost of quality trend and the major cost of quality trend.

Total Cost of Quality (COQ) Trend Chart

NOTE: The blank worksheets in Book Two may be photocopied for your convenience in completing the assignments. Additional copies are available from Hitchcock Publishing Company, Wheaton, IL 60188; phone 312/665-1000.

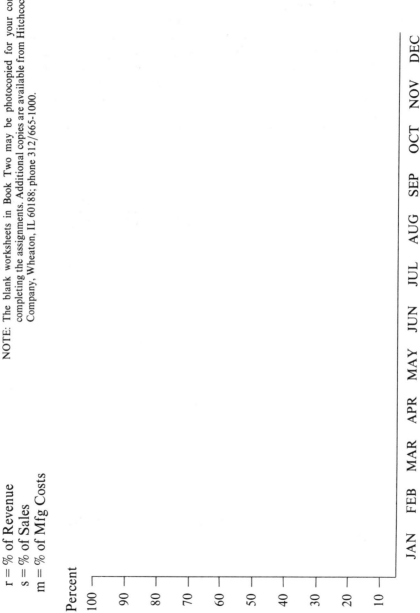

r = % of Revenue
s = % of Sales
m = % of Mfg Costs

Percent
100
90
80
70
60
50
40
30
20
10

JAN   FEB   MAR   APR   MAY   JUN   JUL   AUG   SEP   OCT   NOV   DEC

Analysis

	JAN	FEB	MAR	APR	MAY	JUN	JUL	AUG	SEP	OCT	NOV	DEC
Revenue												
Cost of Sales												
Cost of Mfg												
Cost of Quality												

Cost of Quality as percent of:

	JAN	FEB	MAR	APR	MAY	JUN	JUL	AUG	SEP	OCT	NOV	DEC
Revenue												
Cost of Sales												
Mfg												

NOTE: Multiply all dollar figures by 1,000

Major Cost of Quality (COQ) Trend Chart

NOTE: The blank worksheets in Book Two may be photocopied for your convenience in completing the assignments. Additional copies are available from Hitchcock Publishing Company, Wheaton, IL 60188; phone 312/665-1000.

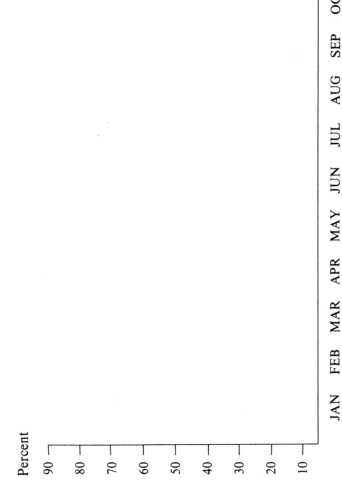

p = Prevention Costs
a = Appraisal Costs
i = Internal Failure Costs
e = External Failure Costs

Percent

90
80
70
60
50
40
30
20
10

JAN   FEB   MAR   APR   MAY   JUN   JUL   AUG   SEP   OCT   NOV   DEC

Analysis

	JAN	FEB	MAR	APR	MAY	JUN	JUL	AUG	SEP	OCT	NOV	DEC
Percentages												
Prevention												
Appraisal												
Internal Failure												
External Failure												

IV. Work Assignment 3
Analysis of Cost of Quality

Situation: You are the new quality director for the Old Line Company. You find that your predecessor had been keeping track of quality costs, but had thrown away all of his data when he cleaned out his desk.

All you have been able to find is his raw data for last year (shown below). Can you make any decisions based on these data?

All data is in thousands of dollars.

Month	Total Revenue	Prevention Costs	Appraisal Costs	Internal Failure Costs	External Failure Costs	Total Cost of Quality
Jan	3,200	15	165	65	450	695
Feb	3,400	15	185	55	430	685
Mar	4,200	25	205	85	570	885
Apr	3,280	5	185	85	460	735
May	3,320	35	205	65	410	715
Jun	4,500	15	215	85	450	765
Jul	3,420	5	200	125	250	580
Aug	3,600	—	175	85	260	520
Sep	4,360	45	215	85	300	645
Oct	3,120	15	175	65	210	465
Nov	3,440	5	175	55	210	445
Dec	3,280	25	185	45	150	405

IV. Work Assignment 4
Analysis of Cost of Quality Data
Analyze the trends of the cost of quality graphs.

Total Cost of Quality (COQ) Trend Chart

r = % of Revenue

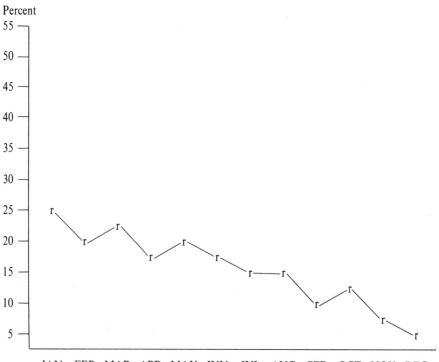

Major Cost of Quality (COQ) Trend Chart

p = Prevention Costs
a = Appraisal Costs
i = Internal Failure Costs
x = External Failure Costs

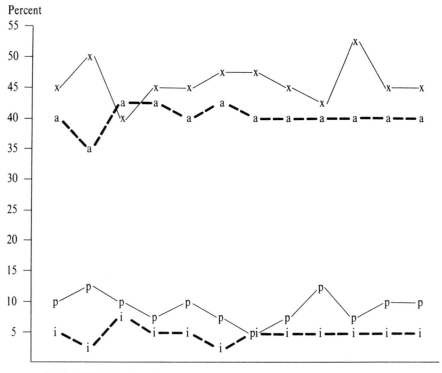

IV. Work Assignment 5
Analysis of Cost of Quality Data
Analyze the cost of quality data shown on the graphs.

Total Cost of Quality (COQ) Trend Chart

m = % of Manufacturing Costs

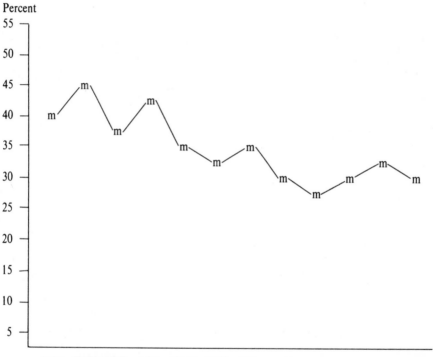

Major Cost of Quality (COQ) Trend Chart

p = Prevention Costs
a = Appraisal Costs
i = Internal Failure Costs
x = External Failure Costs

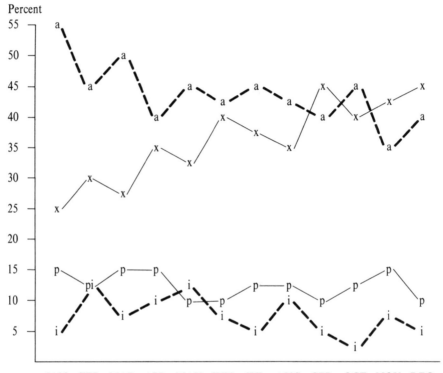

IV. Work Assignment 6
Analysis of Cost of Quality Data
Analyze the cost of quality trends shown on the graphs.

Total Cost of Quality (COQ) Trend Chart

r = % of Revenue

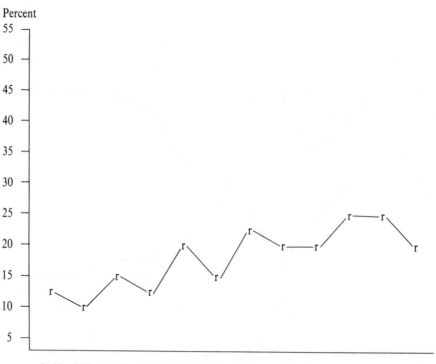

Major Cost of Quality (COQ) Trend Chart

p = Prevention Costs
a = Appraisal Costs
 i = Internal Failure Costs
x = External Failure Costs

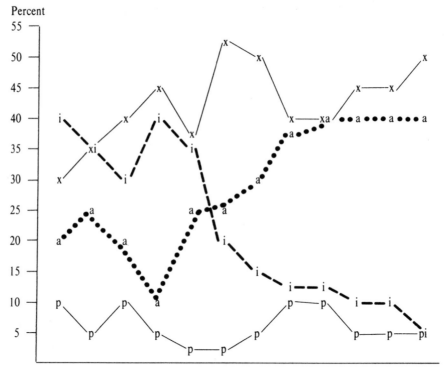

JAN   FEB   MAR   APR   MAY   JUN   JUL   AUG   SEP   OCT   NOV   DEC

Summary of Principles

1. The graph of the total cost of quality displays historical data and makes it easy to verify trends.

2. The graph of the cost of quality categories makes it easy to spot trends and estimate ratios between the four categories.

3. Some rules of thumb for the ratios of the cost of quality:
   a. Total failure costs should be about half of the total cost of quality.
   b. Internal failure cost to external failure cost ratio should be about 1 to 9.
   c. The ratio of appraisal costs to prevention costs should be about 4 to 1.
   d. Each category, in relation to the total cost of quality, will have about the following ratios:

Prevention	1:10
Appraisal	4:10
Internal Failure	1:20
External Failure	9:20

These ratios are offered as guides only. They may not apply to your industry, especially if you are in a business where it is either "zero defects or zero business." It should also be noted that all of these guides are based on the definitions of category as outlined in Book One. The authors advise that comparison with "industry standards" is like using sand for the foundation of a building. Many companies have no idea of the magnitude of their cost of quality and those who do recognize it are usually reluctant to publicize that magnitude.

4. Here are some action item suggestions for ratio imbalances:
   a. Failure costs too high: Look for more efficient prevention and appraisal methods to reduce failure costs with little change in appraisal and prevention costs.
   b. Appraisal costs too high: Use audits or "frugal" sampling to reduce appraisal costs without allowing failure costs to rise.
   c. When cost ratios are in balance, start looking for "breakthrough" areas which will reduce any or all quality cost areas while maintaining or bettering existent quality and reliability levels.

APPENDIX I

Life Cycle Costs
Answers and Comments

I. Work Assignment 1 Answers
Sharing of Excess Life Cycle Costs

a. Based on last year's maintenance costs, $8.5 million, for 213 gasoline-powered trucks, the average truck's maintenance is:

$$\frac{\$8,500,000}{213} = \$39,906 \text{ (or approx. } \$40,000)$$

$$(100 \text{ converted trucks}) \times (\$40,000) \times (10\%) = \$400,000$$

In other words, if everything is as promised, Federal will be able to pay for the conversion of 100 gasoline-powered trucks in the first year of operation. But . . . Federal can save 8 percent on a continuing basis, with no risk and no additional capital, simply by embarking on a program to replace each gasoline-powered truck with diesel as it wears out.

It appears that the decision to install the Electron-John ignition system, based on the above analysis, is a greater risk than warranted by the rewards of the system when compared to diesel conversion, especially since diesel is a known factor for Federal.

b. The appropriate action for Electron-John's marketing people is to sharpen their pencils and make a more attractive offer to Federal if they expect to sell their system.

c. As an outside consultant to Federal, you would probably advise them at this point to switch to diesel. You would advise Electron-John to go back to the drawing board and come up with a higher projected maintenance savings, especially stressing the increased quality of service and enhanced maintenance schedule that this would bring about.

I. Work Assignment 2 Answers
Rebate Based on Excessive Failures

a. Federal's reliability assurance clause may have seemed to be well thought out, but the monthly requirement of 200 hours is pretty stringent and the yearly requirement of 2,400 hours is really too tough.

The monthly requirement of 2 percent or less failures, 200 hours in a month, would require the probability of operation (reliability) for a month to be 98 percent, the equivalent of a mean time between failures (MTBF) of 10,000 hours.* The annual requirement of 5 percent or less failures (2,400 hours) would require the probability of operation (reliability) for a year to be 95 percent, which would be the equivalent of an MTBF of 46,784 hours.

b. If you were working for the supplier bidding on this job, you would take exception to both of the reliability requirements and propose in their place a maintenance program that would give a greater operational availability.

c. As an outside consultant, your recommendation to both Federal and to each prospective supplier would be that they meet and discuss how best to satisfy Federal's needs.

I. Work Assignment 3 Answers
Cost Sharing Based on Degenerative MTBF Trend

On the surface there is nothing wrong with the computer company's request for inclusion of guarantees of Mean Time Between Failures (MTBF) performance as a part of the contract. However, evaluation of the risk indicates that a 10 percent dip below the 15,000-hour MTBF would probably bankrupt OUR Company, since this would amount to a 15 percent return of at least a third of the Company's gross. This risk is minimized though, since the MTBF guarantee requirement is less than half the calculated value.

While the risks are minimal, the following items should be made a part of the contract before OUR Company makes it final decision:

a. OUR Company's reliability people shall review and approve in writing the customer's methods for determining MTBF from actual use field data.

b. The customer's records regarding reliability determination shall be open to OUR Company.

c. To avoid putting OUR Company in financial jeopardy, liability shall be limited to the net profit which results from this contract.

*Refer to the Quality Management Handbook, Chapter 13 (see Bibliography and Recommended Reading, page 84).

OUR Company's books shall be open for any inspections required for such determination of profits.

■ Comments

Further, it should be recommended as a part of any warranty program that OUR Company should be contracted for the determination and administration of the field maintenance program designed to repair or replace OUR Company's product when warranted.

All of these steps will minimize OUR Company's risks but satisfy the intent of the MTBF guarantees asked for in the customer's request for quotation.

I. Work Assignment 4 Answers
Design Review Based on Life Cycle Estimates
Problem 4a: Institution

Following are the calculations for the U.S. Customs facility:

	($ million)
Maintenance cost = (12 years)×($0.8 million)	$ 9.6
Manning cost = (12 years)×($1.45 million)	$ 17.4
1 gate for 12 years	$ 27.0
Cost of 10 gates = ($27 million per gate)×(10 gates)	$270.0
Initial cost of 10-gate facility	$ 27.0
Total Life Cycle Cost for life of facility (12 years) = ...	$297.0

It is immediately clear that the combined maintenance and manning costs for the proposed facility ($270 million over 12 years) are very high in proportion to the cost of building the facility ($27 million). While there are no hard and fast rules, a general rule of thumb or first approximation is that total life cycle costs (acquisition costs plus repairs, maintenance, upkeep etc.) should be around or less than twice acquisition costs. In this example, life cycle costs are 11 times acquisition costs ($297 million/$27 million).

Clearly, the 2 to 1 ratio will not be appropriate for all purchases or projects. For a project with heavy personnel costs—as this problem is—ratios of 5 or 6 to 1 may not be inappropriate. A ratio of 11 to 1, however, strongly indicates that further review is in order.

Several alternatives may be possible. Perhaps more money could be invested in automated or computer controlled equipment at the outset. Suppose, for example, that by adding $3 million in more sophisticated equipment initially, maintenance and manning costs could be reduced by 5 percent. This would result in an initial investment of $30 million, but would reduce life cycle costs by $13.5 million and reduce the ratio to 9.6 to 1 ($270 million—$13.5 million + $30 million/$30 million). Still very high, but better. Even more important, there would be a net saving of $10.5 million ($13.5 million − $3.0 million).

Another alternative might be to build nine gates initially instead of ten. Now, the initial (acquisition) cost would be $24 million and maintenance and manning costs would be $243 million. Total life cycle costs would be $267 million, or $30 million less than the 10 gate facility. The new ratio, however, would be 11.1 to 1, and this might be considered moving in the wrong direction. Note, however, that in this case the $30 million saving would be more than enough to cover the acquisition cost of the facility.

■ Comments

The point of this problem is to show that purchase or acquisition costs are only a part of the overall costs of ownership, and that decisions made during initial study or design can greatly influence how much an owner/user pays over the long run. While life cycle costs and quality costs are different concepts, they must both be understood and controlled to achieve customer satisfaction and company success.

4b: Support Van

a. Since every solution seems to bring an increased initial cost, as well as increased operational and maintenance costs, your agenda should be as follows:
1. Review of all present proposals.
2. Discussion of feasibility:
   • Life cycle cost estimate
   • Risk elements
   • Arrive at consensus
3. Investigate other methods to accomplish task:
   • Other power sources
   • Other kinds of pumps
   • Other innovation
b. Other proposals covering other solutions you might make are:
1. Use of a five-gallon jerrycan which could be connected externally
2. Gravity-feed tank filler with an external funnel in which to pour

the gasoline to fill the tank.

3. Use of a simple hand pump that requires no fuel usage.

■ Comments

Of all the above solutions, perhaps the hand pump is the best solution. It doesn't deviate too far from the original design but still reduces the original costs as well as the total life cycle costs.

APPENDIX II

Cost of Quality Exercises
Answers and Comments

II. Work Assignment 1 Answers
First Estimate of Quality Costs

a. Yes, it is possible to estimate Leptran's quality costs using returned materials and gross sales as the basis. Doubling the returned material costs will normally give you a good estimate of total quality costs. Comparison of the estimated quality costs to gross revenue will give you a very quick indication of how well the company is doing with regard to quality costs.

b. Yes, based on the available information it would appear that there is ample justification to proceed with a quality cost program. The preliminary indications are that Leptran's quality costs are running about $4.2 million per year (or 20 percent of gross revenue) and this certainly represents some opportunity for improvement.

c. Based on a 20 percent improvement in the cost of quality, Leptran's profit will be doubled. The calculations are as follows:

At present:
Gross Revenue	=	$21.100 million
Cost of Quality (20%)	=	4.220 million
Net Profit	=	0.844 million

After improvement:
Gross Revenue	=	$21.100 million
Cost of Quality (16%)	=	3.376 million
Net Profit (8%)	=	1.688 million

■ Comments

It should be noted that in the early stages cost reduction efforts are likely to yield much more than just 20 percent improvement in the cost of quality. Therefore, a reasonable estimate of profit improvement would be a doubling or even tripling of profits.

d. Following are some steps you might propose to initiate a quality cost program for Leptran:

Step 1. Perform preliminary quality cost estimate using data available for returned materials, factory rework, inspection, etc.

Step 2. Analyze and break down cost categories as much as possible based on available data.

Step 3. Identify possible improvement areas that can be quickly attacked to produce immediate cost reductions.

Step 4. Prepare a report to management detailing the preliminary quality cost estimate and address potential improvement areas.

Step 5. Secure management support and proceed with implementation of the quality cost program.

II. Work Assignment 2 Answers
Elementary Cost of Quality Analysis

	Actual Expense	Burden Rate	Total Expense
2a. Prevention Costs = $ 13,860			
Quality Planning	6,300	2.2	13,860
Appraisal Costs = $133,360			
Inspection and Test Wages	23,200	2.2	51,040
Burn-in and Final Test	33,600	2.2	73,920
Audit	2,000	2.2	4,400
Calibration (Outside Lab)	4,000	N/A	4,000
Failure Costs = $254,180			
Material Review Board	700	2.2	1,540
Warranty Reserve	21,000	N/A	21,000
Complaint Adjustment	25,000	2.2	55,000
Repair/Retest Burn-in Failures	22,400	2.2	49,280
Reinspection/Retest of Rework	5,800	2.2	12,760
In-plant Scrap	4,000	N/A	4,000
In-plant Rework	3,000	2.2	6,600
Field Returns	104,000	N/A	104,000

II. Work Assignment 2b Answers

If:

Internal Failure Cost = $ 74,180

Material Review Board	1,540
Repair/Retest Burn-in Failures	49,280
Reinspection/Retest of Rework	12,760
In-plant Scrap	4,000
In-plant Rework	6,600

And:

External Failure Costs = $180,000

Warranty Reserve	21,000
Complaint Adjustment	55,000
Field Returns	104,000

Then:

External Failure Cost Ratio = 180,000 / 74,180 = 2.4

So:

The ratio of
Internal Failure Costs to External Failure Costs
is approximately 1:2

II. Work Assignment 2c Answer

Though this company is profitable, it is only marginally so. Any slight glitch in revenues or manufacturing costs will likely wipe out profits. With estimated quality costs in excess of 18 percent it is clear this company is not as well managed as it ought to be.

On the positive side, it appears there are opportunities for doubling or tripling profits with well-conceived improvement programs.

II. Work Assignment 3a Answer
Cost of Quality (COQ) Analysis (2nd Quarter)

Revenues   6,109,000   Cost of Mfg.   1,193,000   Cost of Sales   2,807,000

| | Actual Expense | Burden Rate | Total Expense | COQ Category as percent of | | | |
				Total Cost of Quality	Revenue	Cost of Sales	Cost of Mfg.
PREVENTION COSTS							
Q E Planning	6,760	2.2	14,872				
Test Engineering	5,070	2.2	11,154				
Reliability Eng.	3,380	2.2	7,436				
Data Acquis. & Analysis	1,690	2.2	3,718				
Total Prevention Costs			**37,180**	**6.2**	**0.6**	**1.3**	**3.1**
APPRAISAL COSTS							
Inspection	20,216	2.2	44,475				
Production Test	31,200	2.2	68,640				
Calibration Service	12,000	—	12,000				
Quality Audit	6,000	2.2	13,200				
Total Appraisal Costs			**138,315**	**23.2**	**2.3**	**4.9**	**11.6**
FAILURE COSTS							
Internal Failure Costs							
Assembly Rework	8,200	2.2	18,040				
ECO Rework	6,384	2.2	14,045				
Inspection Rework	20,800	2.2	45,760				
Test Debug & Rework	2,600	2.2	52,200				
Material Review Board	9,200	—	9,200				
Total Internal Failure Costs			**92,765**	**15.6**	**1.5**	**3.3**	**7.8**
External Failure Costs							
Complaint Adjustment	50,000	2.2	110,000				
Returned Material	154,000	—	154,000				
Warranty Charges	63,000	—	63,000				
Allowances							
Total External Failure Costs			**327,000**	**54.9**	**5.6**	**11.6**	**27.4**
TOTAL FAILURE COSTS:			**419,765**	**70.5**	**6.9**	**15.0**	**35.2**
TOTAL COST OF QUALITY:			**595,260**	**100.0**	**9.7**	**21.2**	**49.9**

NOTE: Sum of percentages may not equal percentage totals due to rounding.

II. Work Assignment 3b Answer
Cost of Quality (COQ) Analysis (1st Quarter)

Revenues 5,719,000   Cost of Mfg. 1,223,000   Cost of Sales 2,863,000

	Actual Expense	Burden Rate	Total Expense	Total Cost of Quality	COQ Category as percent of		
					Revenue	Cost of Sales	Cost of Mfg.
PREVENTION COSTS							
Q E Planning							
Test Engineering							
Reliability Eng.							
Data Acquis. & Analysis							
Total Prevention Costs			40,200	6.0	0.7	1.4	3.2
APPRAISAL COSTS							
Inspection							
Production Test							
Calibration Service							
Quality Audit							
Total Appraisal Costs			155,440	23.2	2.7	5.4	12.7
FAILURE COSTS							
Internal Failure Costs							
Assembly Rework							
ECO Rework							
Inspection Rework							
Test Debug & Rework							
Material Review Board							
Total Internal Failure Costs			104,520	15.6	1.8	3.7	8.5
External Failure Costs							
Complaint Adjustment							
Returned Material	335,000	—	335,000				
Warranty Charges							
Allowances							
Total External Failure Costs			367,830	54.9	6.4	12.8	30.1
TOTAL FAILURE COSTS:			472,350	70.5	8.3	16.5	38.6
TOTAL COST OF QUALITY:			670,000	100.0	11.7	23.4	54.8

NOTE: Sum of percentages may not equal percentage totals due to rounding.

Note: Total cost of quality is estimated at two times the value of field-returned materials. Distribution of costs are based on average ratios taken from 2nd quarter data.

II. Work Assignment 3c Answer
Total Cost of Quality Trend Chart

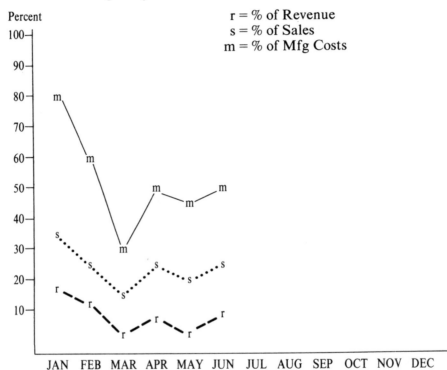

	Jan	Feb	Mar	Apr	May	Jun
Revenues	1,757	1,767	2,195	1,920	1,889	2,300
Cost of Sales (COS)	875	884	1104	834	873	1,100
Cost of Mfg.	387	371	465	382	261	450
Cost of Quality (COQ)	312	222	136	188	165	242
Cost of Quality:						
as % of Revenue	17.8	12.6	6.2	9.8	8.7	10.5
as % of COS	35.7	25.1	12.3	22.5	18.9	22.0
as % of Mfg	80.6	59.8	29.2	49.2	45.7	53.7

Note: Multiply all dollar figures by 1,000.

II. Work Assignment 3d Answer
Major Cost of Quality Trend Chart

p = Prevention Costs
a = Appraisal Costs
 i = Internal Failure Costs
e = External Failure Costs

Percent

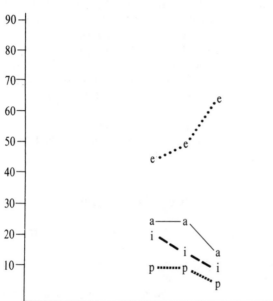

JAN FEB MAR APR MAY JUN JUL AUG SEP OCT NOV DEC

	Apr	May	Jun
Prevention	7.4	7.2	4.7
Appraisal	26.6	26.7	18.3
Internal Failure	18.7	17.4	11.9
External Failure	47.3	48.7	65.1

Note: The ratios of the major cost categories for January, February and March could be estimated by averaging the ratios from April, May and June. While this might improve the appearance of the chart, the data would be highly speculative and of little real value.

II. Work Assignment 3e Answer

a. We have been tracking the cost of quality within our manufacturing facility since January of this year.

b. Initially, the cost of quality started at about 18 percent in January, and declined in both February and March. This was followed by a slight increase in cost of quality (COQ) in the period between April and June, but in general COQ has averaged about 10.7 percent over the last two quarters for which there is data.

c. In analyzing the distribution of costs among the four major cost categories (prevention, appraisal, internal failures, and external failures), it is clear that external failure costs are way out of line with what would be expected under optimal performance conditions.

d. During the past six months almost $700,000 has been spent in external failure costs and about $200,000 in internal failure costs. During the same period the company made an estimated profit of about $475,000 which is just over half as much as was spent on failure costs.

e. These data clearly indicate that enormous savings and ultimately increased profits would result from a minimal investment in a cost of quality improvement program.

II. Work Assignment 3f Answer

a. Develop and/or refine cost of quality data collection techniques with the aid of accounting staff.

b. Prepare and issue monthly cost of quality (COQ) reports detailing cost trends and performance.

c. Establish steering committee consisting of representatives from all major organizations within the company.

d. Establish sub-committees (task force) to research and implement corrective actions for major cost items based on Pareto analysis of problem areas.

e. Report regularly to management on progress and obstacles affecting improvement activities.

f. Continue these efforts until cost of quality categories are balanced and there are no apparent improvement projects that will do better than break even.

g. Review the program and start over when appropriate.

APPENDIX III

Pareto Analyses and Matrices
Answers

III. Work Assignment 1 Answer
Graph: Pareto Analysis

Percent

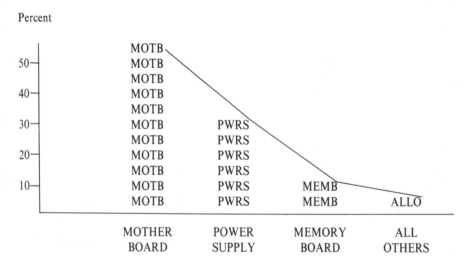

III. Work Assignment 2 Answer
Graph: Cumulative Pareto Analysis

Percent

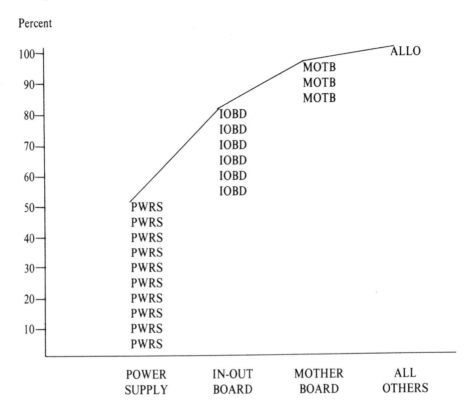

III. Work Assignment 3a-1 Answer
Simple Matrix

Assembly		1	2	3	4	5	6	7	8	9	10	11	12	13	14	15	16
Mother Board	(39)		8		14	5	2				10						
Power Supply	(24)						1	1					5			17	
Memory Board	(19)	6		2			9			2							
All others	(9)	1	2	1	1	1	1	1		1							
Total	(91)	7	10	3	15	6	12	2	1	3	10		5			17	

III. Work Assignment 3a-2 Answer
Graph: Cumulative Pareto Analysis

Percent

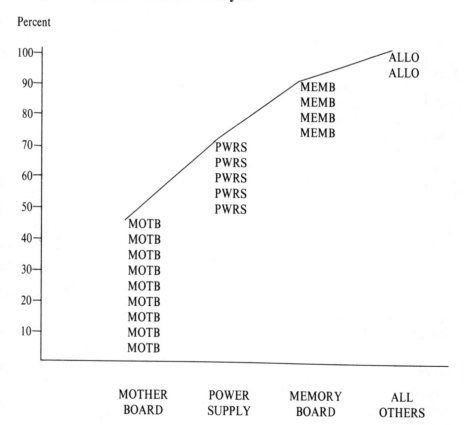

III. Work Assignment 3a-3 Answer
Graph: Cumulative Pareto Analysis

Percent

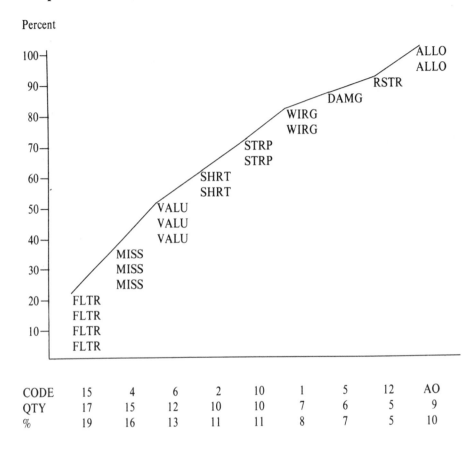

CODE	15	4	6	2	10	1	5	12	AO
QTY	17	15	12	10	10	7	6	5	9
%	19	16	13	11	11	8	7	5	10

III. Work Assignment 3b-1 Answer
Simple Matrix

Cost Factor		1	2	3	4	5	6	7	8	9	10	11	12	13	14	15	16
Mother Board	(164)		16		70	30	8				40						
Power Supply	(130)							1	5				5			119	
Memory Board	(118)	54		6			36			22							
All others	(43)	9	4	3	5		4	1		11							
Total	(455)	63	20	9	75	36	48	2	5	33	40		5			119	

III. Work Assignment 3b-2 Answer
Graph: Cumulative Pareto Analysis

Percent

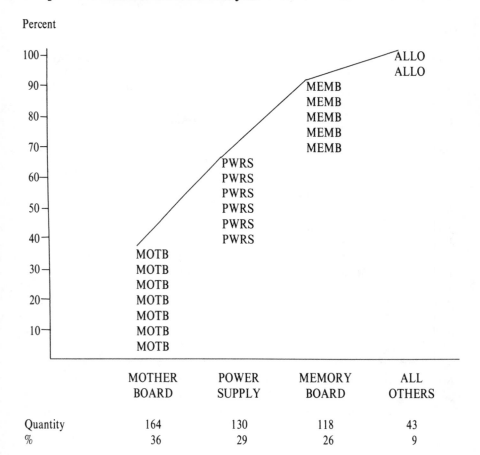

	MOTHER BOARD	POWER SUPPLY	MEMORY BOARD	ALL OTHERS
Quantity	164	130	118	43
%	36	29	26	9

III. Work Assignment 3b-3 Answer
Graph: Cumulative Pareto Analysis

Percent

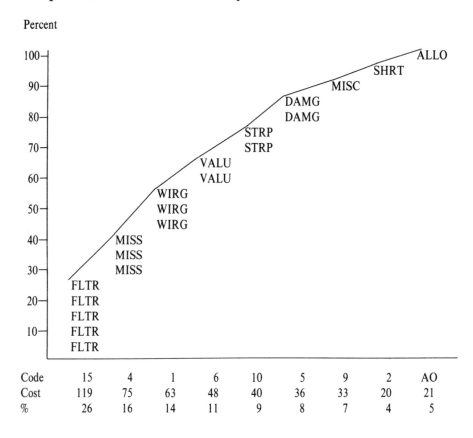

Code	15	4	1	6	10	5	9	2	AO
Cost	119	75	63	48	40	36	33	20	21
%	26	16	14	11	9	8	7	4	5

III. Work Assignment 3c-1 Answer
Simple Matrix

Criticality		1	2	3	4	5	6	7	8	9	10	11	12	13	14	15	16
Mother Board	(96)		16		56	10	4				10						
Power Supply	(97)							2	5				5			85	
Memory Board	(66)	18		4			18			26							
All others	(32)	3	4	2	4	2	2	2		13							
Total	(291)	21	20	6	60	12	24	4	5	39	10		5			85	

III. Work Assignment 3c-2 Answer
Graph: Cumulative Pareto Analysis

Percent

```
100 ┤                                          ALLO
                                              ALLO
 90 ┤                              MEMB
                                   MEMB
 80 ┤                              MEMB
                                   MEMB
 70 ┤                              MEMB
                     MOTB
 60 ┤                MOTB
                     MOTB
 50 ┤                MOTB
                     MOTB
 40 ┤                MOTB
         PWRS
 30 ┤    PWRS
         PWRS
 20 ┤    PWRS
         PWRS
 10 ┤    PWRS
         PWRS
```

	POWER SUPPLY	MOTHER BOARD	MEMORY BOARD	ALL OTHERS
CF	97	96	66	32
%	33	33	23	11

CF = Criticality Factor — refers to the frequency of occurrences.

III. Work Assignment 3c-3 Answer
Graph: Cumulative Pareto Analysis

Percent

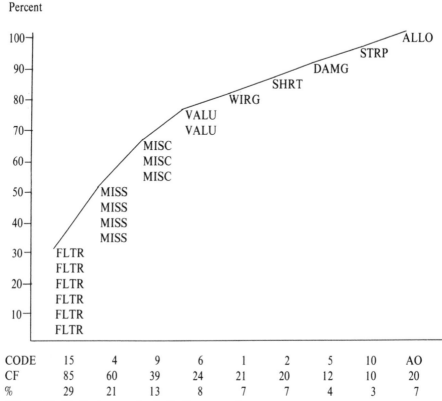

CODE	15	4	9	6	1	2	5	10	AO
CF	85	60	39	24	21	20	12	10	20
%	29	21	13	8	7	7	4	3	7

CF = Criticality Factor — refers to the frequency of occurrences.

III. Work Assignment 4 Answers
Freelance Pareto Analysis

a) When undertaking Pareto analysis by failure cause, avoid the narrow view and look at "the big picture." Look at the scrap costs in this problem, for example.

1. Items 1 and 6 are both engineering changes and total $25,900, accounting for 43 percent of the total scrap cost.

2. Items 2, 3 and 4 are all bad finish and total $20,903, which is 35 percent of the total scrap cost.

3. The bad welds and rust category is a far-behind third in our

Pareto analysis, at $5,708 or 9.55 percent of the total scrap cost.

b) Corrective action

Engineering changes — 43 percent — $25,900

1. Institute a rigorous design review on all new items.

2. Begin a tolerance review of all items already in production.

3. Review "use as is" dispositions resulting from Material Review Board (MRB) actions.

Bad Finish — 35 percent — $20,903

1. Investigate handling procedures and practices for all skins and covers.

2. Review finish processing procedures.

3. Review MRB actions concerning scrap items due to bad finish.

Bad Welds, Rust — 9.6 percent — $5,708

1. Review welding and finish procedures for frames.

2. Review handling and storage procedures and practices.

3. Review MRB actions with regard to scrapped frames.

c) Justifying the corrective action plan:

1. *Engineering changes:* Since most changes are due to oversight in the design phase, a rigorous design review will prevent many mistakes from "going to the floor." Similarly, any mistakes that haven't been caught yet may be eliminated with less cost by catching them in a re-review process. Looking for "use as is" dispositions usually will show where tolerances are too tight or just plain wrong. Correcting this situation will at least prevent the cost of the MRB actions needed to "buy off" engineering's mistakes.

2. *Bad Finish:* Most bad finishes are caused by mishandling. This is, therefore, a most fertile area for corrective action. However, you can't overlook the possibility that you are doing something wrong at the outset and that's the reason for this choice. Reviewing the scrap actions may give you better insight into areas that you have overlooked.

3. *Bad Welds, Rust:* You have to look at the whole process because you're either doing something wrong in handling or in storing. Cover all bets and then review the scrap actions and you may find something you've missed before.

d) An appropriate message to management might be:

Dear Boss:
Back me in this program and I will cut 40 percent ($24,000) out of our scrap cost by the end of the year—and I'll do it with the people that I already have on board.
Yours with best Quality in mind,
Quality Manager

APPENDIX IV

Cost of Quality Analyses
Answers and Comments

IV. Work Assignment 1 Answers
Analysis of Interruption of Manufacturing
■ Comments:

It is hard to determine trends from the fluid graph fluctuations resulting from the break and restart of manufacturing for this company, but there are two things which may be concluded. First, the total cost of quality before and after the "break" was never much lower than 10 percent of revenue. Second, the ratios of the cost of quality categories are out of balance.

■ Recommendations:

1. Now that the system has had at least a few months to stabilize, it is time to look around to see what makes our appraisal category so high. Perhaps we are over-inspecting. Maybe we could replace an "inspection gate" with an "audit" or several audits with a roving inspector. There are many recommendations that we might make, but they could all be generalized under *Work smarter—not harder!*

2. At the same time, we should be looking at our internal failures. Why are they so high compared to our external failures? A few Pareto analyses and lots of hard work and attention to detail should pay great dividends.

3. Reducing the costs of appraisal, with no reduction in effectiveness, and bringing down the costs of internal failures will do much toward balancing this company's quality costs.

4. Bringing about balance as listed in recommendation 3, will also bring about a reduction of the total quality cost, with a corresponding increase in profit.

IV. Work Assignment 1
Total Cost of Quality Trend Chart

r = % of Revenue
s = % of Sales
m = % of Mfg Costs

Percent

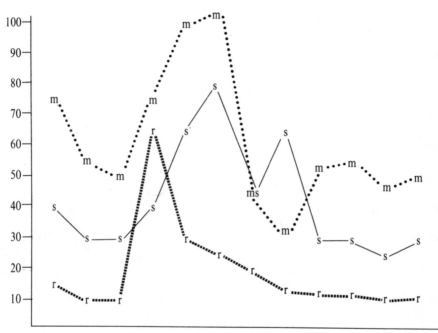

	Jan	Feb	Mar	Apr	May	Jun	Jul	Aug	Sep	Oct	Nov	Dec
Revenues	8.46	10.58	15.09	2.08	5.02	7.82	7.57	10.58	14.92	12.74	12.77	16.97
Cost of Sales (COS)	3.38	4.23	6.04	3.45	2.01	2.01	3.03	2.12	5.97	5.10	5.11	6.82
Cost of Mfg.	1.69	2.12	3.02	1.72	1.24	1.56	3.03	4.23	2.99	2.55	2.56	3.39
Cost of Quality (COQ)	1.28	1.10	1.48	1.31	1.24	1.64	1.32	1.31	1.63	1.32	1.16	1.65
Cost of Quality:												
as % of Revenue	15.2	10.4	9.8	62.9	24.8	20.9	17.4	12.4	10.9	10.4	9.1	9.7
as % of Sales	37.9	26.0	24.5	38.0	61.9	81.3	43.5	61.8	27.4	25.9	22.8	24.1
as % of Mfg.	75.8	52.0	49.1	76.3	100.1	104.6	43.5	30.9	54.7	51.8	45.6	48.5

NOTE: Multiply all dollar figures by one million.

IV. Work Assignment 1, continued
Major Cost of Quality Trend Chart

p = Prevention Costs
a = Appraisal Costs
i = Internal Failure Costs
e = External Failure Costs

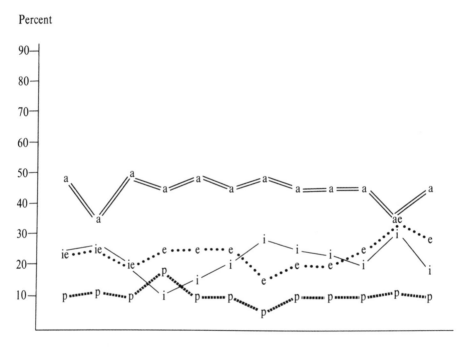

	Jan	Feb	Mar	Apr	May	Jun	Jul	Aug	Sep	Oct	Nov	Dec
Prevention	9.5	11.1	10.2	17.3	9.7	9.4	8.7	9.3	9.1	9.1	10.4	9.3
Appraisal	47.1	37.8	50.1	44.1	48.8	45.4	46.2	45.1	45.4	45.5	36.5	45.5
Internal Failure	21.8	25.7	19.7	11.9	16.7	19.8	28.5	25.7	23.6	20.9	20.0	17.7
External Failure	22.1	25.4	20.0	26.6	24.8	25.5	16.6	20.0	21.9	24.5	34.0	27.4

IV. Work Assignment 2 Answers
Analysis of a New Company's Cost of Quality
Total Cost of Quality Trend Chart

m = % of Mfg Costs

Percent

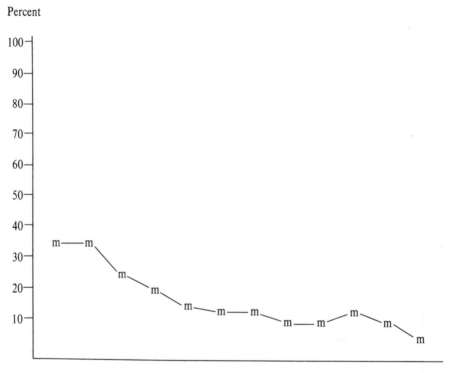

	Jan	Feb	Mar	Apr	May	Jun	Jul	Aug	Sep	Oct	Nov	Dec
Cost of Mfg.	1.4	1.65	2.45	1.88	2.12	2.7	2.54	2.72	3.28	2.48	2.62	3.06
Cost of Quality (COQ)	0.45	0.55	0.61	0.36	0.35	0.36	0.35	0.31	0.36	0.34	0.28	0.24
Cost of Quality: as % of Mfg.	32	33	25	19	17	13	14	11	11	14	11	8

NOTE: Multiply all dollar figures by one million.

IV. Work Assignment 2 Answers, continued
Analysis of a New Company's Cost of Quality
Major Cost of Quality Trend Chart

p = Prevention Costs
a = Appraisal Costs
 i = Internal Failure Costs
 e = External Failure Costs

Percent

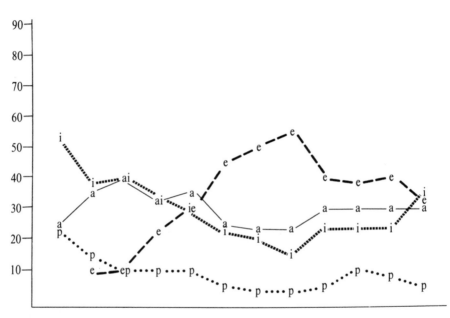

Percent (%):	Jan	Feb	Mar	Apr	May	Jun	Jul	Aug	Sep	Oct	Nov	Dec
Prevention	22	16	10	11	9	6	3	3	6	9	7	4
Appraisal	27	35	39	33	34	28	26	26	31	29	29	29
Internal Failure	53	38	41	33	29	25	20	16	25	24	25	33
External Failure	—	9	10	22	29	42	51	55	39	38	39	33

IV. Work Assignment 2, continued
■ Comments:
1. Although the total cost of quality as a percentage of the cost of manufacturing shows a beautiful trend, it also presents a slight worry.

   a. What does it mean? How beneficial is the trend?

   b. Unless we have historical data we really have no way of evaluating how beneficial it is.

2. The graph for the individual cost of quality categories swings so wildly that it is hard to determine trends from it. An educated guess based on the last three months supports an imbalance that has the failure costs at about 70 percent of total with the ratios between internal and external similarly out of balance. The ratio between prevention and appraisal costs are closer to optimum, but they too are still off.

■ Recommendations:
Since the failure cost categories seem to be 70 percent more or less, of the total quality costs it is reasonable to conclude that the overall figure will go down when more money is spent on appraisal. However, additional appraisal tasks should be approached in a scientific manner.

1. Use Pareto analysis or other methods to determine the most fruitful areas to find savings.

2. Establish your plan to reduce the "target" failure costs.

3. Estimate probable savings and use this figure to justify any appraisal costs.

4. Present your proposal to management in language that they will understand.

5. Pursue your project to bring total quality cost into line.

6. Use your initial successes in your overall program as a spur to continue your pursuit of quality cost reduction.

7. Add your own ideas to those given here (they may be even better) and you too will find that quality pays.

IV. Work Assignment 3 Answers
Analysis of Cost of Quality

r = % of Revenue

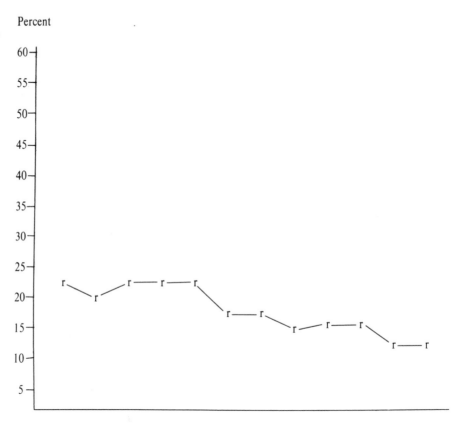

Percent

	Jan	Feb	Mar	Apr	May	Jun	Jul	Aug	Sep	Oct	Nov	Dec
Revenues	3.2	3.4	4.2	3.28	3.32	4.5	3.42	3.6	4.36	3.12	3.44	3.28
Cost of Quality (COQ)	.695	.685	.885	.745	.715	.765	.580	.520	.645	.465	.445	.405
Cost of Quality: as % of Revenue	22	20	21	23	22	17	17	14	15	15	13	12

NOTE: All costs are in millions of dollars.

IV. Work Assignment 3 Answers, continued
Analysis of Cost of Quality

p = Prevention Costs
a = Appraisal Costs
 i = Internal Failure Costs
 e = External Failure Costs

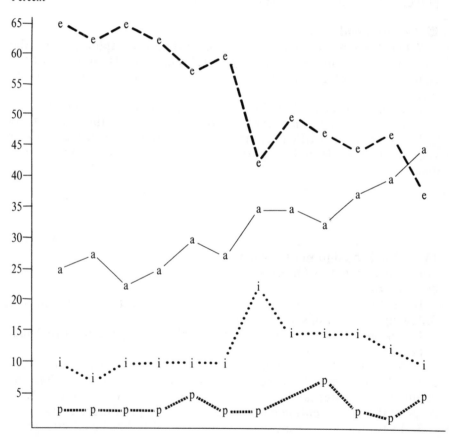

Percent (%):	Jan	Feb	Mar	Apr	May	Jun	Jul	Aug	Sep	Oct	Nov	Dec
Prevention	2	2	3	1	5	2	1	—	7	3	1	6
Appraisal	24	27	23	25	29	28	34	34	33	38	39	46
Internal Failure	9	8	10	11	9	11	22	16	16	14	12	11
External Failure	65	63	64	62	57	59	43	50	47	45	47	37

IV. Work Assignment 3 Answers, continued
Analysis of Cost of Quality
■ Comments:

Everything seems to be right with this company. There has been about a 50 percent reduction in their total cost of quality (as a percent of revenue) for the year shown and the ratios of all of their quality costs seem to have been brought into line by the last three months of the year. However, it appears that the ending cost of quality (12 percent of revenue) could be improved upon.

■ Recommendations:

When the costs of quality are balanced (see Chapter 8), i.e., the costs of failure amount to half the total quality costs, your efforts to continue the total cost of quality on its downward trend should include:

1. Look for projects to reduce the total cost of quality even more.
2. Look for reduction of the costs required to maintain this control.
3. Use more statistical control for the same confidence level in your control while reducing the total amount of inspection being done.

IV. Work Assignment 4 Answers
Analysis of Cost of Quality
■ Comments:

In analyzing the cost of quality graphs in this problem, the following observations are in order:

1. The general trend for the cost of quality, as a percent of revenue, appears to be beneficial.
2. Quality costs were high (20 or 25 percent) at the first of the year although, in general, they were balanced. Appraisal to prevention was about 4 to 1. Internal failure to external failure was about 1 to 9. Appraisal plus prevention costs were about equal to failure costs.
3. In twelve months the overall cost of quality has been reduced to about 5 percent of revenue.
4. Evidently, this company is making good progress in making quality pay.
5. It is obvious that everyone in this company has had a share in improving quality and productivity!

Note: The total cost of quality graph was shown only as a percent of revenue to make any trends easier to visualize.

■ Recommendations:

It is worth repeating that when the costs of quality are balanced (see Chapter 8), i.e., the costs of failure amount to half the total quality costs—your efforts to continue the total cost of quality on its downward trend should include the following tasks:

1. Look for projects to reduce the total cost of quality even more.

2. Continue to look for reductions of the costs required to maintain this control.

3. Use more statistical control for the same confidence level in your control while reducing the total amount of inspection being done.

IV. Work Assignment 5 Answers
Analysis of Cost of Quality
■ Comments:

In analyzing the cost of quality graphs for this work assignment, the following observations can be made:

1. The general trend for the cost of quality, as a percent of manufacturing costs, appears to be beneficial.

2. Total cost of quality was about 40 percent of manufacturing costs at the first of the year, then went down to about 30 percent at year's end.

3. From the major cost of quality trend chart, the ratios of the individual categories of quality costs indicate too much emphasis on appraisal early in the year, culminating in what appears to be an almost optimum balance in December.

4. Evidently, this company has a well-defined quality cost program in place and it is functioning well in their quest to make quality pay.

5. It is possible that we have misread the data, since there are other factors that could affect manufacturing costs. Suppose for instance, that manufacturing costs have risen during the year. This could account for the apparent beneficial trend for the total quality cost graph. While the probability is high, perhaps 90 percent, that our interpretation of the trend is correct, it can easily be verified by using a second index. In this case, it would probably be best to graph the total cost of quality as a percentage of revenue for more accurate determination of just how good our quality improvement is.

Note: The total cost of quality graph is indexed only as a percent of manufacturing costs to make any trends easier to visualize. In this case, we really need at least one more index for comparison.

IV. Work Assignment 6 Answers
Analysis of Cost of Quality
■ Comments:

In analyzing the cost of quality graphs in this problem, the following observations are in order:

1. The general trend for the cost of quality, as a percent of revenue, appears to be rising (from about 12 percent to about 20 percent.) In our analysis of the cost of quality trends, we see that this might be the result of an increased appraisal effort which has been successful (more or less) in balancing the categories. The final aim of this strategy, of course, is to lower cost of quality, but this is still in the future.

2. Quality costs, while lower at the first of the year were far out of balance. Appraisal to prevention was about 2 to 1. Internal failure to external failure was about 1 to 1. Appraisal plus prevention costs to failure costs were about 1 to 3.

3. In twelve months the overall cost of quality has almost doubled.

4. Analysis of the individual cost of quality categories would indicate that additional time and effort [cost] has been invested in appraisal in order to successfully reduce the costs of internal failure. This has increased the overall quality cost (as a percentage of revenue) but the end result is that the quality costs are now balanced. Now, continued reduction of the total quality cost should be a continuing process.

5. It is obvious that everyone in this company has shared (and is continuing to share) in a long term effort to improve quality and productivity!

INDEX

Acceptability of the product 15
Acceptable performance limits 63
Accounting procedure 72
Acquisition costs 125
Action item 49, 50
  group 46
  method 31
Actual quality costs 20, 21, 32
Administrative activities 61
Advertising cost 17
Aerospace companies 52-53
Allocation
  cost of quality 21
  overhead expenses 22
Allowances 7, 17
Analysis and planning account code 74
Analysis of costs 31
Analyzing costs 66, 71
Applied life cycle cost principles 9
Appraisal costs 6-7, 10, 15, 33, 38, 40, 53,
    55, 57-60, 63, 82
  activities 62
  chart of accounts 64
  codes 73, 75-77, 81, 82
  field test costs 81
  regulatory agency evaluations 81
  vs. prevention costs 31, 60
  worksheets, sample 68
Avoidable quality costs 17, 26, 32, 33

Basic work 62
Burden rate 22-24, 36, 72, 93, 128
  as a multiplier 23
  as an adder 23
  calculation 22-24
  estimate 22-23
  for subcategories 23
  overhead 22, 23, 61
  ratio 22

Calibration
  contracts 15
  cost 15
  /maintenance 7, 15
  services 36
  system 15
Categories of quality costs 14, 63
Certification of vendors 53
CF—see Criticality Factor
Charge codes 12
Charge sorting system 19
Chart of quality cost accounts 12
Charting quality costs 30
Clerical activities 61

Clerk 61
Closure date 49
Closure documentation 50
Code numbers 28-29
Collecting, collection of quality costs 11,
    19-24
Company philosophy 67
Comparability 63
Comparison standard 32
Complaint adjustment 7, 17
Computer workstations 9
Conformance to design 10
Conformance to specification 7
Continuous quality verification 53
Control charts 63
Controlling quality costs, white collar 61-65
COQ - Cost of Quality—see Quality costs
Corrective action 31, 49, 50
Cost-effective improvement program 44
Cost categories 6-7, 14, 21, 25, 33, 52
Cost of appraisal—see Appraisal costs
Cost of design—see Quality costs
Cost of external failures—see External
    failures
Cost of
  finding defects 58
  internal failures—see Internal failures
  prevention—see Prevention costs
  quality—see Quality costs
  reduction program 35, 65
  sales 57
Cost-sharing based on product failures 9, 88, 123
Costs of
  failure 8
  lack of quality control 6, 7
  quality control 6,7
Costs related to quality 4
  —see also Quality costs
Cover letter 35, 37, 63, 66
Criticality Factor 141, 142
Crosby, Philip B. 84
Customer allowances (external failure) 64
Customer complaint adjustment (external
    failure) 64
Customer needs, ability to meet 15
Customer satisfaction 4
Customer's requirements 14

Data
  acquisition 7, 36
  analysis 64
  collection 11, 14
Debug 36
Defect descriptions example 28-29, 103
Defense Contract Administrative Services
    (DCAS) 5

Deficiencies of:
  design 16
  materials 16
  parts 16
  processes 16
  workmanship 16
Definitions 11, 12, 71
Deming, W. Edwards, Dr. 3, 4, 84
Department activity logs 62
Design quality 7-8
Design review based on life cycle 89, 124-125
Detailed cost summary 35, 38, 40, 65
Detailed trend charts 66
Development of standards 21
Diminishing returns 48
Direct labor 22
Discounts 17
Distribution plan, monthly report 65
Double the company's profit 5
Downtime (internal failure) 64

ECO—see Engineering change order
Engineering change order (ECO) 36
Engineering labor account codes 80-82
Errors, white collar 61-62
Estimating appraisal costs 36
Estimating quality costs 20, 72
Estimating, synthesizing data 92-94
Expense for quality assurance 72
External failure costs 6-7, 10, 36, 38, 55, 57, 59, 63, 79-80, 82-83
  activities 62
  chart of accounts 64
  codes 73, 79-80, 82-83
  customer allowances 64
  customer complaint 64
  end user costs 79
  field failure reporting 80
  field technical assistance 81-82
  OEM costs 79-80, 81
  product liability costs 80
  ratio to internal failure 31, 60, 121, 154
  reprocessing 64
  reproofing 64
  spares carrying cost 80
  spares usage cost 80
  worksheet, sample 70
External rework 16
External to internal failure cost ratios 31, 60, 121, 154

Failure cost categories 31
Failure cost factor —see Failure costs
Failure costs 6-7, 16, 19, 20, 28, 33, 36, 38, 40, 41, 53, 54-57, 59, 63, 64, 70
  worksheet sample 70
Failure costs too high 54-57, 59

Feigenbaum, Armand V. 84
Field
  data 22
  engineering costs 7
  equipment calibration 76
  failure costs 7
  inspection and test 77
  service account codes 82
Final acceptance 15
First estimate of quality costs 20-21, 91, 127
First-time appraisal 36
First-time manufacture 21
Follow-up date 49
Follow-up responsibility 49
Formal statement of implementation 50
Formal statement of verification 50
Freelance Pareto analysis 107
Frugal sample plans 53
Fuel consumption 9

Gantt charting 48
General labor account codes 74-80
General ledger 20
General quality costs 14
General trend for cost of quality 54
Good will costs 16, 17
Graphic sales tool 66
Graphical presentation 65
Graphing quality cost data 25, 32

Harrington, H.J. 62, 84
Heiland, R.E. 84
Historical and trend data 59
Hourly rates 36

Implementation date 49
Implementing the improvement process 46-49
Improvement process 51
Improvement program 44-51
In-process inspection 15
Incoming inspection 15, 68
Increased productivity 10
Index for quality costs 30-31
Indices for quality costs 30-31
Indirect labor salaries 23
Industry standards 31
Inspection
  cost 15
  rework 16
  procedures 7, 14
  test (appraisal) 68
  test code 75, 77
Internal failure costs 6-7, 10, 26, 36, 38, 57, 59, 63, 64, 82
  activities 62
  chart of accounts 64

codes 73, 77-79, 81, 82
corrective action 78-79
defective product 78-79
downtime 64, 78-79
handling and transportation 78
investigate defect cause 78, 81
material value 78
MRB activities 79, 81
ratio to external failure 31, 60, 154
reprocessing 64
reproofing 64
rework 78
scrap costs 77
transportation costs 78
vendor failure costs 78
wages and salary costs 78
worksheet, sample 70
Internal rework 16
Internal to external failure cost ratios 31, 59, 60, 121
Interpretation of quality cost data 12
Interruption of manufacturing 108, 144

Japan 3, 32
Juran, J.M. 84

Labor
    costs 20, 83
    distribution 20, 21
Laboratory expenses 15
Laboratory testing code 75
"Learning tool" 10
Legitimate quality cost 66
Life cycle costs 8-10, 86-90, 122-126
Life cycle optimization 9
Life testing 15
Line engineer 20
Lot sampling 53
Luxurious designs 10

Maintenance
    appraisal 64
    cost 15
Major categories of quality costs 6-7, 30, 63
Major cost factors 63
Major cost of quality trend chart 40, 55, 57, 59, 98-99, 112-113, 116, 118, 120, 133, 146, 148
Management
    commitment 44
    report 35
    support 67
Managing the improvement process 48-51
Manpower development 74-75
Manufacturing calendars 20
Manufacturing costs (as index) 30

Material
    control 21
    costs 20
    expenses 22
    review actions 16
    review board (MRB) 7, 16, 36, 72
Matrices, matrix 28-29, 33
Mean Time Between Failures (MTBF) 88, 123
Measure white collar quality costs 62
Measuring performance, white collar 63
Medical device makers 53
MIL-Q-9858A 4
MIL-STD-105 53
Minimizing appraisal costs 14
Minimizing failure costs 14
Minimum performance standards 62
Monthly report 65, 72
MRB—see Material review board
MTBF—see Mean Time Between Failures

Net profit (as index) 30
Normal trends 32-33
Normalizing quality costs 30
Notable quality cost trends 66

OEM—see Original equipment manufacturer
Operating costs 6, 8, 20
    environment 13
    statement 20
Operational quality costs 7, 10
Optimization 52
Optimizing profits 53
Optimum cost of quality 52
Optimum total quality cost 52
Organizing and managing for improvement 44-51
Original equipment manufacturer (OEM) 79-80, 81, 83
Out-of-calibration problems 15
Outside endorsement costs 77
Overhead
    burden rate 61
    costs 22
    expenses 23

Pareto
    analysis, analyses 25-29, 39, 41, 47, 66, 101-107
    examples 26-29, 101-107
    freelance analysis 107
    matrices, matrix 28-29, 33, 101-107
    "Pareto-ize" 29, 31
    presentation 40
Percent of manufacturing costs 57-58
Percent of revenue 54, 56

Perfect product 53
Periodic reports 66
Personal logs 62
PERT (Project Evaluation and Reporting
    Technique) 48
Pharmaceutical companies 53
Poor Quality Cost 62, 84
Prepare job specification 64
Prevention costs 6-7, 10, 14-15, 36, 38, 40,
    53, 55, 57, 59, 60, 63, 71, 80-81, 82
  activities 62
  audit cost account 80
  chart of accounts 64
  codes 73, 74-75, 80-81, 82
  manufacturing process 80
  pre-production product test 81
  product planning 80
  quality and reliability test equipment 80-
    81
  tasks 36
  vs. appraisal costs 31, 60
  worksheet, sample 69
Printed circuit board 9
Probables (causes) 31
Problem statement 49
Procedure, quality cost 13
Process control
  analysis 74
  audits 74
  certification 74
Product design verification 75
Production inspection and test 76
Production test 15
Productivity 4
Profit improvement 5, 6, 25, 35, 36, 39,
    40, 61
Profit picture 36
Program review 50
Project Evaluation and Reporting
    Technique (PERT) 48
Proofing (appraisal) 64
Proposals for corrective action 65
Purpose, statement of 11-12, 71

Quality assurance
  clerical 76
  department 71
  process test 76
Quality audit 7, 15, 76-77
Quality control clerical and supervisory
    costs 76
Quality Control Handbook 84
Quality control inspection 76
Quality costs 4, 5, 6, 7, 20
  account codes 64, 73
  account structure 74-83
  accounting 21, 72
  accounting data 22
  accounting reports 22
  accounts 12, 64, 73

accounts chart 64
analysis of- 25-34, 37, 94-95, 108-121,
    130-131, 147-148, 150-154
as percentage of revenue 20
categories of- 6-7, 14, 21, 25, 33, 52
chart of accounts 64
codes 21
comparison 32
compiling data 25
concept 7, 71
data 19, 25, 71
design 7-8
definition 14, 71
display 28
estimating 20, 21
graphs 54-60
index for- 30-31
indices for- 30-31
optimal 53
overhead costs 22, 25
percentage allocation of hours or dollars
    21
procedure 11-13, 71-73
program 5, 10, 19, 25, 32, 33
ratios of- 31
reducer 46
relationship 52
reporting of data 12, 19, 32, 33, 35-43
sources for- 24
subcategories 6-7, 25, 63
summary 72
systems 21
tabular presentation 25
tabulation 25, 66
total cost 20
training 32
trend charts 54-59, 72, 96-97, 110-111,
    115-120, 132-133, 145-148
trends 63, 154
white collar- 61-65
worksheets, sample 68-70
Quality
  improvement 10
  information costs 15
  information equipment 75-76
  information systems 15
  planning 7, 14, 72
  policy 14
  program 4,5
  reliability 9
  system audit 64
  system planning 64
  training 47, 74
Quality Is Free 84
Quality magazine 84
Quarterly program review 50

Random-time sampling 62
Ratio of failure costs to prevention and
    appraisal costs 60, 121

Ratio of prevention cost versus appraisal
    cost 60, 121
Rebate based on excessive failures 87, 121
Redesign 9
Reducing the costs of quality 66
Reducing white collar overhead 61-65
Reference section 11, 12
Referencing related documents 12
Reinspection 7, 15, 20, 36
Relative costs 72
Reliability engineering 7, 15
Reliability task 36
Reliability testing 15
Repair cost 15, 16, 20
Report formats 35, 63
Report white collar costs, how to 63-65
Reporting of quality cost data 12, 71
Reporting of results to management 50
Reporting trends 19
Reprocessing (internal/external failure) 64
Reproofing (internal/external failure) 64
Retest 7, 15, 20
Retrofit 9
Return on investment study 56
Returned material 7, 17
    allowances 21
Review customer order 64
Rework costs 7, 16, 20, 21
Richardson, W.J. 84

Sales cost (as index) 30
Sales revenue (as index) 30
Sample report 35-43
Sampling 58
Scope, statement of 11-12, 71
Scrap costs 7, 20
Screening 100 percent 58
Self-analysis 62
Semiconductor users 58
Service sector 61
Sharing excess life cycle costs 8-9, 86, 122
Skip lot sample 53
Smoothing the data 30-31
Sources for quality costs 24
Specification, quality information
    equipment 74
Spot trends 25
Spread of probabilities 58
Statement of purpose 11-12
Statement of scope 11-12
Statistical Control of Quality, The 84
Statistical process control 53, 58-59, 63

Statistical quality control 58-59
Subcategories of quality costs 6-7, 25, 63
Supervisor 20

Table of quality costs 31
Tabular presentation 25
Target dates 50
Task force 45-46
Test 7
    debug and rework 28
    engineering 7, 15
    inspection of purchased material 75
Testing of rework 16
Three-month rolling average 30-31, 56
Total cost of quality trend chart 39, 54, 56,
    58, 96-97, 110-111, 115, 117, 119,
    132, 145, 147
    failure costs 20
    life costs 10
    use costs 8
Total Quality Control 84
Total use costs 8
Totally free of defects 14
Tracking improvement activities 48
Training cost 7
Training programs 14
Trend charts 35, 65
Trend line, favorable 67
Tuning the quality cost system 52

Use cost 8
    —See also Life cycle costs

Warranty costs 7, 16
White collar
    cost accounts 64
    errors 61-62
    how to measure costs 62-65
    how to report costs 63-65
    overhead 61-65
    quality costs 61-65
Word processing equipment 62
Word processing services cost accounts 63-
    64
Work order
    reporting 21
    system 21
Work Sampling 84